U0085026

編者的話

　　克漏字測驗（ *Cloze Test* ）是在最短的考題當中，以等距離挖空方式，徹底測驗出學生的真正程度。它具有三大優點：

1. 綜合閱讀選擇、閱讀填充等多變化題型。
2. 徹底測驗出學生用詞（ *usage* ）、成語、文意、文法（ *grammar* ）、推理等多種實力。
3. 強調通盤了解並須融會貫通，引導英文教學的正確方向。

✄ 掌握聯考趨勢・配合新編教材 ✄

　　根據歷屆聯考及最新聯考趨勢顯示，克漏字測驗已成為英語科必考題型。針對這種必然的趨勢，我們精心編寫「**國中英語 100 分克漏字測驗**」，使您掌握聯考英語科得分關鍵。

　　基於高中及五專聯考絕不超出課本範圍的原則，本書內容完全配合國中最新教材編寫，題目最具代表性。將國中六冊課文改編成**基礎篇**，奠定基礎。網羅各校月考、模擬考、及與聯考同一來源的資料，編成**實力篇**，加強實力。

　　本書共分二部分，Part I 包含基礎篇和實力篇 80 個 Tests；Part II 蒐集 80 到 85 年度北聯、省聯及北、中、南區五專聯招試題，內容充實。每個 Test 和每份試題，都有標準答案、詳細的解說和中譯，收錄在**國中英語 100 分克漏字測驗詳解**中。本套書是老師出題，學生練習的最好選擇，更為準備聯考的最佳利器。

　　本書無論編撰或校稿，都秉持著審慎的態度，但仍恐有疏漏之處，尚祈各界先進不吝批評指教。

CONTENTS

Editorial Staff

- 編著 / 王榮一

- 校訂 / 劉　毅・蔡琇瑩・謝靜芳・吳濱伶・莊心怡

- 校閱 / Edward C. Yulo ・ Tina W. Leggett
  John C. Didier　・ Bruce S. Stewart
  John H. Voelker ・ Kenyon T. Cotton

- 封面設計 / 張鳳儀

- 版面設計 / 張鳳儀

- 版面構成 / 張鳳儀・吳正順・蘇淑玲

- 打字 / 黃淑貞・吳秋香

PART·I

基礎篇〔Test 1~Test 56〕
實力篇〔Test 57~Test 80〕

1 [第一册] 第 1~5 課

時間：20分鐘 ＊ 得分：　／15分

A 請仔細閱讀下面文章，選出最適當的答案，使句意完整。

> *Tom* : Stand up!
>
> *Students* : Good morning, Miss Wang.
>
> *Miss Wang* : ____1____, students. How are you today?
>
> *Students* : ____2____ .
>
> *Tom* : Sit down.
>
> *Miss Wang* : Jean, ____3____ . ____4____ that picture. ____5____ is that?
>
> *Jean* : It is a chair.
>
> *Miss Wang* : Very good. Thank you. Sit down, please.

1. (　) ① Good morning ② Good afternoon
      ③ Good evening ④ Good luck
2. (　) ① Fine thank you ② Fine, thank you
      ③ Thank you ④ Thank you, fine
3. (　) ① please, stand up ② Stand up please
      ③ please stand up ④ Stand up please
4. (　) ① See ② See at ③ Look ④ Look at
5. (　) ① How ② Who ③ What ④ Where

B 請仔細閱讀下面文章，將最適當的一個字填入空格中。

John　：　___6___　your name?

Mary　：　My name is Mary.

John　：　Please s__7__ the word "Mary."

Mary　：　M-a-r-y, "Mary."

John　：　___8___　is that tall boy?

Mary　：　That is Bill.

John　：　Is he your brother?

Mary　：　No, he ___9___ . He is not my brother.

John　：　Is he a ___10___ student?

Mary　：　Yes, he is a good student.

6. ＿＿＿＿＿＿

7. ＿＿＿＿＿＿

8. ＿＿＿＿＿＿

9. ＿＿＿＿＿＿

10. ＿＿＿＿＿＿

Miss Li　：　Are you a student, Bill?

　　Bill　：　Yes, I am a ___11___ .

Miss Li　：　Notice（留意）that s__12__ t girl. ___13___ her name?

　　Bill　：　Her name is Sue.

Miss Li　：　Is she a teacher?

　　Bill　：　No, she is not. She is not a teacher. She is a student, ___14___ .

Miss Li　：　Thank you. Good-bye.

　　Bill　：　___15___ .

11. ＿＿＿＿＿＿

12. ＿＿＿＿＿＿

13. ＿＿＿＿＿＿

14. ＿＿＿＿＿＿

15. ＿＿＿＿＿＿

2 [第一冊] 第 6~10 課

時間：20分鐘 ✱ 得分：　　／15分

A 請仔細閱讀下面文章，選出最適當的答案，使句意完整。

Mother : ____1____ is your father, Sue?

Sue : He is in the living room and is reading a book.

Mother : ____2____ is your brother doing?

Sue : He is writing English words.

Mother : ____3____ two glasses on the table?

Sue : Yes, there are. There are two glasses on the table.

Mother : Is your sister ____4____ school?

Sue : Yes, she is.

Mother : Is there a blackboard in her classroom?

Sue : Yes, there is. There is one ____5____ the wall.

1. (　　) ① What　　② When　　③ Where　　④ How

2. (　　) ① What　　② When　　③ Where　　④ How

3. (　　) ① Is there　　　　　② Are there
　　　　 ③ There is　　　　 ④ There are

4. (　　) ① at　　② with　　③ on　　④×

5. (　　) ① at　　② in　　③ on　　④×

B 請仔細閱讀下面文章，將最適當的一個字填入空格中。

Tom : Is your cat ___6___ the living
        room?

Mary : ___7___ , it is not.

Tom : ___8___ is it?

Mary : It is in the park.

Tom : There are two cats n___9___
        the park. They are running and
        playing. Is your cat blue?

Mary : ___10___ , my cat is black.

6. _____

7. _____

8. _____

9. _____

10. _____

Father : ___11___ is your mother?

Jean : She is in the kitchen.

Father : What is she doing?

Jean : She is c___12___ .

Father : Where is your sister?

Jean : She is sleeping ___13___ the
        sofa.

Father : Is your brother watching
        television?

Jean : Yes, he is watching TV
        ___14___ the living room.

Father : ___15___ are those girls near
        the door?

Jean : They are my classmates.

11. _____

12. _____

13. _____

14. _____

15. _____

③ [第二册] 第 **1・2** 課

時間：20分鐘 ✿ 得分：　　／10分

A 請仔細閱讀下面文章，選出最適當的答案，使句意完整。

John : Are you a teacher?

Bob : ___1___ I am not. I am not a teacher. I am a new student in the class.

John : My name is John. ___2___ your name?

Bob : My name is Bob.

John : How old are you?

Bob : I am ___3___ . How old are you?

John : I am eleven years old.

Bob : My sister is eleven, ___4___ .

John : ___5___ time is it?

Bob : It is nine o'clock in the morning.

1. (　) ① Yes, 　　② No. 　　③ No, 　　④ Yes.

2. (　) ① What's 　②Is it 　③ Isn't it 　④ How's

3. (　) ① twelve 　　　　②twelve old
　　　　　③ twelve year old 　④ years in twelve

4. (　) ① neither 　② either 　③ too 　④ nor

5. (　) ① How 　② What 　③ Which 　④ Where

B 請仔細閱讀下面文章，將最適當的一個字填入空格中。

Mary : Who is number 1?

Jean : He is my brother.

Mary : What is his name?

Jean : His name is John.

6. _____

Mary : How ___6___ is he?

7. _____

Jean : He is ten years old.

8. _____

Mary : I am ten, too. What is John doing?

9. _____

Jean : He is sleeping ___7___ his room.

10. _____

Mary : What time is it?

Jean : It is eight ___8___ in the morning.

Mary : Is your sister ___9___ home?

Jean : Yes, she is. She is studying English in her room.

Mary : What is your father doing?

Jean : He is e___10___ breakfast.

[第二冊] 第 **3.4** 課

時間：20分鐘 ＊ 得分：　　/10分

A 請仔細閱讀下面文章，選出最適當的答案，使句意完整。

Jim : Hello, Bill.

Bill : Hi, Jim. ＿＿＿1＿＿＿ are you？

Jim : Fine, thank you. How are you？

Bill : Fine, thanks. ＿＿＿2＿＿＿ are you going？

Jim : I am going to school.

Bill : Do you speak English？

Jim : Yes, ＿＿＿3＿＿＿.

Bill : Does your sister speak English？

Jim : Yes, she does. She speaks ＿＿＿4＿＿＿.

Bill : What time is your first class？

Jim : It ＿＿＿5＿＿＿ at eight-ten. What time is it？

Bill : It is eight o'clock.

1. (　　) ① What ② How ③ Who ④ Which

2. (　　) ① What ② Where ③ How ④ Which

3. (　　) ① a little ② little ③ a few ④ few

4. (　　) ① English good ② good English
　　　　 ③ good a English ④ a good English

5. (　　) ① works ② begin ③ is ④ starts

B 請仔細閱讀下面文章，將最適當的一個字填入空格中。

Peter : Hi, Tom. Do you walk to school every day?

Tom : Yes, I do. What is Jonh ___6___?

Peter : He is talking ___7___ his friend, Bill.

Tom : Where is your sister going?

Peter : She is going to the park.

Tom : Are ___8___ flowers and birds in the park?

Peter : Yes, there are.

Tom : Do you have a ___9___ sisters?

Peter : Yes, I do. I have two sisters.

Tom : Do they ___10___ television every day?

Peter : Yes, they do.

6. _____

7. _____

8. _____

9. _____

10. _____

5 [第二冊] 第**5·6**課

時間：20分鐘 ＊得分： ／15分

A 請仔細閱讀下面文章，選出最適當的答案，使句意完整。

Sue : What time do you get up every morning？

Mary : I ___1___ get up at five o'clock every morning.

Sue : You get up very early！

Mary : What time do you eat breakfast？

Sue : I eat breakfast at seven in the ___2___ .

Mary : What time does your class begin？

Sue : At eight-ten in the morning.

Mary : What time does your father ___3___ ？

Sue : At six-thirty in the afternoon.

Mary : ___4___ does your sister do？

Sue : She is a teacher. She teaches Music ___5___
a school.

1. (　) ① seldom　② don't　③ usually　④ hardly

2. (　) ① home　② morning　③ noon　④ evening

3. (　) ① came home　② go to home
　　　 ③ go bed　④ come home

4. (　) ① What　② How　③ What's　④ How's

5. (　) ① at　② on　③ of　④ for

B 請仔細閱讀下面文章，將最適當的一個字填入空格中。

George Wang is the boss of a big company in our t 6 . P 7 e of this area（地帶）like to be his friends, because he is always kind and generous（慷慨的）to others. His son is now t 8 n and studies in a j 9 high school. They l 10 in the country.

6. _____

7. _____

8. _____

9. _____

10. _____

My grandfather works on the farm every day. He is a _____ 11 . Though he is now seventy, he is b 12 all day on the farm. He g 13 corn（穀類）on his farm, and sometimes he harvests（收穫；收成）v 14 es. During my summer vacation, I always go to h 15 Grandfather.

11. _____

12. _____

13. _____

14. _____

15. _____

⑥ [第二冊] 第 *7·8* 課

時間：20分鐘 ＊ 得分： ／15分

A 請仔細閱讀下面文章，選出最適當的答案，使句意完整。

Peter：What day is today?

Tom：It's Sunday. It's the last day ____1____ the week.

Peter：The last day? It's the first day.

Tom：No! Sunday is the last day. Monday is the first day.

Peter：Yes, ____2____ the calendar. There are seven days ____3____ a week. They are Sunday, Monday, Tuesday, Wednesday, Thursday, Friday, ____4____ Saturday. Sunday is the ____5____ day; Saturday is the last day.

1. (　) ① of ② on ③ in ④ by

2. (　) ① look ② look over
　　　③ look in ④ look at

3. (　) ① on ② in ③ of ④ by

4. (　) ① or ② but ③ except ④ and

5. (　) ① first ② second ③ third ④ fourth

B 請仔細閱讀下面文章，將最適當的一個字填入空格中。

There are four ___6___ in a year. Spring comes ___7___ winter and it is very warm in spring. In summer, it is very hot. Fall comes ___8___ winter and it is c ___9___ in fall. The l ___10___ season of the year is winter. In winter, it is very cold.

6. _____

7. _____

8. _____

9. _____

10. _____

Teacher : What day don't you go to school?

Student : ___11___ . It's the first day of the week.

Teacher : Yes. And ___12___ is the first season of the year?

Student : It's ___13___ . Spring is a warm season.

Teacher : Right. Do you know the names of the four seasons ___14___ a year?

Student : Yes. They are spring, ___15___ , fall, and winter.

11. _____

12. _____

13. _____

14. _____

15. _____

[第二冊] 第 *9・10* 課

時間：20分鐘 ＊ 得分：　　／15分

A 請仔細閱讀下面文章，選出最適當的答案，使句意完整。

Bill : Did you have class yesterday?

Tom : Yes, I had.

Bill : Weren't you ＿＿1＿＿ school yesterday?

Tom : ＿＿2＿＿ . I was sick.

Bill : Where were you?

Tom : I was ＿＿3＿＿ home all day.

Tom : What did you do yesterday?

Bill : ＿＿4＿＿ Lesson Nine.

Tom : ＿＿5＿＿ it easy?

Bill : Yes, it was easy. Will you have an English test tomorrow?

Tom : Yes, I will have an English test, so I want to go home to study.

1. (　　) ① in　　② going to　　③ going for　　④ on
2. (　　) ① No, I was not.　　② Yes, I was not.
　　　　③ Yes, I was.　　④ No, I was.
3. (　　) ① at　　② in　　③ on　　④ by
4. (　　) ① I studied　　② I was studying
　　　　③ Yes, I studied　　④ No, I was studying
5. (　　) ① Was　　② Is　　③ Does　　④ Do

B 請仔細閱讀下面文章，將最適當的一個字填入空格中。

Mary was not in school yesterday. She was s___6___ . She stayed in bed all day. Her sister did many things ___7___ the morning. She was very b___8___ .

Mary : Did you clean the rooms ?

Jane : No, I ___9___ . I washed my skirt.

Mary : Did you i___10___ it ?

Jane : Yes, I did.

6. _____

7. _____

8. _____

9. _____

10. _____

___11___ was Sunday yesterday. Mary ___12___ very busy in the morning. She h___13___ her mother wash the rice and the vegetables. Then she c___14___ lunch. After lunch she talked w___15___ her sister.

11. _____

12. _____

13. _____

14. _____

15. _____

8 [第二冊] 第 11·12 課

時間：20分鐘 ✱ 得分：　　/15分

A 請仔細閱讀下面文章，選出最適當的答案，使句意完整。

The most beautiful places in the cities are the parks. People like to be close to the tall trees and beautiful

flowers in the parks. We can _____1_____ many people in the parks. On holidays, I often play _____2_____ and eat lunch there. _____3_____ lunch, I will always _____4_____ my trash, and put it in the trash bag（袋）. I always _____5_____ .

1. (　　) ① see ② saw ③ seen ④ seeing

2. (　　) ① the tennis ② frisbee
　　　　③ the frisbee ④ a tennis

3. (　　) ① At ② After ③ Before ④ On

4. (　　) ① put away ② pick up
　　　　③ throw away ④ put up

5. (　　) ① liked ② enjoyed
　　　　③ have good times ④ have a good time

B 請仔細閱讀下面文章，將最適當的一個字填入空格中。

Yesterday was Sunday. John got up early. He ___6___ breakfast at six. After breakfast, he ___7___ to many places. At seven-thirty he went to the zoo ___8___ bus. He saw many animals there. There ___9___ many tigers, monkeys, and birds. ___10___ last, he went home at eleven o'clock.

6. _____

7. _____

8. _____

9. _____

10. _____

It was Saturday yesterday. Our family ___11___ a picnic in the zoo. We got up very early, and then went there on a bus. We talked and laughed ___12___ the bus. At twelve-ten, we ate our lunch in a r___13___ near the zoo.

11. _____

12. _____

13. _____

14. _____

15. _____

There are many a___14___ in the zoo. We sang many songs and played. Before we went home, we threw our trash into the trash c___15___.

9

[第三冊] 第 **1** 課

時間：20分鐘 ＊ 得分： /10分

A 請仔細閱讀下面文章，選出最適當的答案，使句意完整。

Among（在～之中）my neighbors, the family that I like best is the Wang family. Mr. Wang had worked in a factory. He was once a factory ___1___ . Now he keeps a store. He goes to his store ___2___ motorcycle. Mrs. Wang is a nurse. She works in a ___3___ . She goes to work by bus. They both like their work. Mr. and Mrs. Wang ___4___ a son and a daughter. They study in an elementary school（小學）. They both ___5___ .

1. (　) ① work　　② works　　③ worker　　④ worked
2. (　) ① on　　② with　　③ by　　④ for
3. (　) ① hotel　　② hospital　　③ shop　　④ kitchen
4. (　) ① has　　② have　　③ had　　④ having
5. (　) ① walks to school　　② walks to the school
　　　　③ walk to school　　④ walk to the school

B 請仔細閱讀下面文章，將最適當的一個字填入空格中。

A boy and a girl who are c＿＿6＿＿
are talking about the fire that broke out
（發生）from the building in ＿＿7＿＿
of Mary's ＿＿8＿＿ last night.

Boy : Was there nobody in the building
when the fire broke out?

Girl : Yes, there was nobody in the
building last night.

Boy : Who was the first one to find
the fire?

Girl : I guess that "he" was Mary's dog,
because he barked all night and
bothered（困擾）some people.
When they woke up, they found
the fire.

Boy : Where is the dog?

Girl : ＿＿9＿＿ in the back of the
house. If you look at him, he
will bark ＿＿10＿＿ you.

6. ＿＿＿＿＿＿

7. ＿＿＿＿＿＿

8. ＿＿＿＿＿＿

9. ＿＿＿＿＿＿

10. ＿＿＿＿＿＿

10 [第三册] 第 2 課

時間：20分鐘 ＊ 得分：　　／10分

A 請仔細閱讀下面文章，選出最適當的答案，使句意完整。

There is an American student in my class. My friends are interested in him. His parents live ___1___ ___2___. He ___3___ to Taiwan last year. He can ___4___ good Chinese. Because he is kind to others, he has many friends here.

My neighbors John and Mary are Americans, too. Their parents live in Germany. John and Mary came to Taiwan ___5___. They can't speak any Chinese. They are studying Chinese in Taipei now.

1. (　) ① on ② at ③ in ④ ×
2. (　) ① Amarica ② Amerika
　　　 ③ America ④ Americe
3. (　) ① comes ② come ③ came ④ comed
4. (　) ① say ② speak ③ tell ④ told
5. (　) ① last week ② in last week
　　　 ③ at last week ④ in week last

B 請仔細閱讀下面文章，將最適當的一個字填入空格中。

John : Mary, who is ___6___ ?

Mary : That's Joe. He is in my class
   this semester（學期）

John : Is he ___7___ American?

Mary : Yes, he is.

John : Did he study Chinese?

Mary : No, he didn't study any Chinese.
   He came to Taiwan last week.

John : Does he ___8___ a bicycle to
   school every morning?

Mary : Yes, he does.

John : Can he ___9___ a car?

Mary : No, he can't.

John : Does he like to play f_ 10 _e?

Mary : I don't know.

John : Can you ask him?

Mary : No, I can't.

John : Why not?

Mary : I can't speak English!

6. _____

7. _____

8. _____

9. _____

10. _____

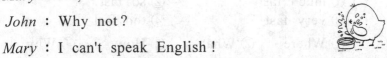

11 [第三冊] 第 **3** 課

時間：20分鐘 ✽ 得分： ／15分

A 請仔細閱讀下面文章，選出最適當的答案，使句意完整。

Betty works in a company. She has to ____1____ a typewriter every day. Though she can type ____2____, she found the typewriter slow. She is now talking with Alice about their work.

Betty : I usually use a typewriter, but I sometimes use a computer. The typewriter is too slow.

Alice : I sometimes use the computer, too. I go to a computer class in the evening.

Betty : ____3____ do you go to class?

Alice : I always go on foot.

Betty : Can I go to your computer class, too?

Alice : Of course, you can. You can start class ____4____ . ____5____ .

1. (　　) ① uses ② use ③ useless ④ used

2. (　　) ① much fast ② so fast
　　　　 ③ very fast ④ too fast

3. (　　) ① Where ② What ③ How ④ Why

4. (　　) ① in this evening ② the evening
　　　　 ③ at this evening ④ this evening

5. (　　) ① We can together go ② We can go together
　　　　 ③ We can go to together ④ We can together go to

B 請仔細閱讀下面文章，將最適當的一個字填入空格中。

Mary Jones works in a large company ___6___ Taipei. She is now a s ___7___ . She likes her work and she is very diligent（勤勉的）. She n ___8___ goes home before seven in the evening from Monday to Friday. She s ___9___ works on Saturdays, b ___10___ she never works on Sundays.

6. _____

7. _____

8. _____

9. _____

10. _____

Mary had a house n ___11___ Taipei. She doesn't live there on Sundays, because she always goes back to her parents' home in Taichung. Sometimes she drives her car to Taichung（台中）, ___12___ sometimes she goes by t ___13___ n . The two vehicles（交通工具）are f ___14___ . She doesn't ride her bicycle for traveling long distances. This is because bicycles are too ___15___ .

11. _____

12. _____

13. _____

14. _____

15. _____

12 [第三册] 第 **4** 課

時間：20分鐘 ✻ 得分：　　／15分

A 請仔細閱讀下面文章，選出最適當的答案，使句意完整。

David and Kevin are classmates. They both go to school ____1____ . Kevin often goes to David's house after school. Sometimes they study together, and sometimes they ____2____ in the park. They usually like to study ____3____ . ____4____ , they always eat lunch ____5____ a good restaurant. On holidays, they also like to have a picnic with their friends. David and Kevin are good friends.

1. (　　) ① by bicycles　　　　② by bicycle
　　　　③ on bicycle　　　　　④ by a bicycle

2. (　　) ① play frisbee　　　　② play a frisbee
　　　　③ play the frisbee　　　④ play frisbees

3. (　　) ① in the evening in the library
　　　　② at the evening in the library
　　　　③ in the library in the evening
　　　　④ at the library in the evening

4. (　　) ① At the weekend　　　② In the weekend
　　　　③ For the weekend　　　④ On the weekend

5. (　　) ① on　　　② at　　　③ in　　　④ upon

B 請仔細閱讀下面文章，將最適當的一個字填入空格中。

My uncle George has a farm near a lake. And ____6____ his farm he has some d__7____ , cats and dogs. One day during the weekend, I went to his farm ____8____ my little brother, with a quack-quack here, a meow-meow there, and e__9__e a bark-bark. O ! We almost couldn't talk ____10____ him.

6. _____

7. _____

8. _____

9. _____

10. _____

A : Do you sometimes ____11____ a computer ?

B : Yes, I ____12____ . I sometimes use a computer.

A : Do you ever use a computer in school ?

B : No, I don't. I ____13____ use a computer in school.

A : And do you always talk ____14____ computers with your brother ?

B : No, seldom（很少）. My brother knows little ____15____ computers.

11. _____

12. _____

13. _____

14. _____

15. _____

13 [第三冊] 第 **5** 課

時間：20分鐘 ✱ 得分： ／15分

A 請仔細閱讀下面文章，選出最適當的答案，使句意完整。

Peter : What are you going to ___1___ this Sunday?

Linda : I'm going to see a movie "Mission: Impossible"
（不可能的任務）. Can you go with me?

Peter : Of course, the movie is very interesting. But
who is ___2___ third person you will invite?

Linda : I will ask John. He is a movie fan（電影迷）.
We often go to the movies together.

Peter : Why don't you ask Bill first? He is also a
movie fan.

Linda : I want to learn English by watching foreign（外
國的）movies, and ___3___ need your help.

Peter : Maybe I can help you a little, though. I don't
___4___ the words said on the movies sometimes. They are too fast. But we'll ___5___
if we go together.

1. ( ) ① have　　② do　　③ be　　④ make
2. ( ) ① this　　② the　　③ one　　④ a
3. ( ) ① I'l　　② I'ill　　③ I'll　　④ I'd
4. ( ) ① Undestand　　② understend
　　　③ undarstend　　④ understand
5. ( ) ① be funny　　② have a fun
　　　③ have fun　　④ have funny

B 請仔細閱讀下面文章，將最適當的一個字填入空格中。

T　6　w is a holiday. Mr. Wang is
not going to work, but Mrs. Wang will.
Mr. Wang will visit his friend living in
the suburbs（郊外）by m　7　e in
the morning. In the afternoon, he will
work in the g　8　n .

Their daughter, Alice, will go to the
m　9　 . Their son is going to go
to a football g　10　 .

The day 　11　 yesterday was
a holiday. I didn't go to school, but
my sister did. I played football on
the playground（運動場）of the park
with my friends in the morning. After
l　12　 , I w　13　 a football game
on t　14　n . In the evening, I went
to a concert（音樂會）and 　15　 a
good time.

6. _____

7. _____

8. _____

9. _____

10. _____

11. _____

12. _____

13. _____

14. _____

15. _____

14 [第三冊] 第 6 課

時間：20分鐘 ＊ 得分： ／10分

A 請仔細閱讀下面文章，選出最適當的答案，使句意完整。

A : Do you feel better today?

B : No, I don't. I feel ___1___ .

A : Did you go to see a doctor?

B : Yes, I did. And I ___2___ some medicine the doctor had prescribed (開藥方) for me. But I still don't feel good.

A : Did you drink a lot of water today?

B : Yes, I drank a lot of water.

A : Did you eat much today?

B : No, I didn't. I only ate little fruit. Did the teacher give us much ___3___ today?

A : No, he only gave us ___4___ .

B : Why?

A : Because many students were ___5___ school today.

1. (　) ① fine　② worse　③ well　④ good
2. (　) ① eat　② took　③ take　④ had
3. (　) ① work　② homeworks　③ homework　④ job
4. (　) ① much　② few　③ a little　④ a few
5. (　) ① absent　② present
　　　 ③ present from　④ absent from

B 請仔細閱讀下面文章，將最適當的一個字填入空格中。

It is possible（有可能的）for people
to ___6___ a cold in each season, but
when the temperature（溫度）fluctuates
（變動）widely in a day, people are
especially apt to be sick. On these
days, some people don't wear enough
clothes in the warm morning and
when they come home in the cool
evening they are not feeling very good
already.

Mary unfortunately（不幸地）caught
a cold yesterday, when she went out
___7___ her friends in the morning.
She wore a s ___8___ r , but she didn't
wear a coat. She came home in the
evening and didn't feel good. Mary
stayed ___9___ home today and had
a rest. She also ___10___ a lot of
water. Now she feels good.

6. _____

7. _____

8. _____

9. _____

10. _____

15 [第三冊] 第 7 課

時間：20分鐘 ＊ 得分：　　　/10分

A 請仔細閱讀下面文章，選出最適當的答案，使句意完整。

Bill : O! How many books ___1___ ! Are they all
yours?

George : No, they aren't. Some are ___2___ and some
are my brother's. Now some of them are
___3___ to us, so we want to sell some.

Bill : How can I help you?

George : Here is a box. You can begin ___4___ here.
You can put these books in this box. I'll
begin ___4___ there.

Bill : Aren't these two books mine?

George : No, they aren't. My father bought them for
me two years ago. They are mine.

Bill : ___5___ is your brother? Won't he help?

George : Of course, he will. He·went to the shops near
here to buy a big box, because these boxes
are too small. Those are his things over there.

1. (　) ① are they ② are there ③ there are ④ they are
2. (　) ① mine ② yours ③ hers ④ their
3. (　) ① useful ② use ③ usefully ④ useless
4. (　) ① to ② on ③ over ④ in
5. (　) ① Where ② Who ③ What ④ Which

B 請仔細閱讀下面文章，將最適當的一個字填入空格中。

Mr. and Mrs. Wang are planning to m __6__ . They don't like the a __7__ t which they live in and will sell it. They will buy a new one near the suburbs （市郊）. Mr. and Mrs. Wang need a house in a residential area（住宅區）. Theirs is now quite near the b __8__ s area. A house with two bedrooms is suitable（合適的）for them, because they have only two little children.

A couple（一對夫妻）looked at the Lins' house this month. They have only one child and liked the house. Because the house is near the m __9__ ns and it has a large garden, the house is very good __10__ the couple. They are going to buy the house.

6. _____

7. _____

8. _____

9. _____

10. _____

16 [第三冊] 第 **8** 課

時間：20分鐘 ＊ 得分： ／15分

A 請仔細閱讀下面文章，選出最適當的答案，使句意完整。

A : Do you play basketball every day?

B : No, we usually play basketball ___1___.

A : Will you play any basketball ___2___?

B : Yes, we will. Will ___3___ join us?

A : Yes, ___4___ will join you.

B : All right! We'll have a team match and we'll have much fun.

A : ___5___ !

B : Good-bye!

1. (　) ① on the weekends　② on weekends
　　　　③ on a weekend　　④ in weekends

2. (　) ① in the tomorrow evening
　　　　② in tomorrow evening
　　　　③ tomorrow evening
　　　　④ in the evening in tomorrow

3. (　) ① you and your friends
　　　　② your friends and you
　　　　③ both you and you friends
　　　　④ your friends and you both

4. (　) ① I and my friends　　② my friends and I
　　　　③ both I and my friends ④ my friends and I both

5. (　) ① Tomorrow see you!　② To see you tomorrow!
　　　　③ See you tomorrow!　④ You see tomorrow!

B 請仔細閱讀下面文章，將最適當的一個字填入空格中。

Last Sunday, I bought a doll ____6____ a present for my sister. I had been thinking about what present I should buy ____7____ several days. After visiting some department stores, I saw a beautiful doll in a small shop. My sister likes dolls very much, so I bought the doll ____8____ her.

____9____ my sister's birthday, I was very excited (興奮的) ____10____ day long. My sister liked the present very much. We had a very good time. I went to bed very late that night.

6. _____

7. _____

8. _____

9. _____

10. _____

David is Helen's brother. They both often discuss (討論) their homework with each other. They usually have ____11____ of homework to do.

Yesterday they ____12____ dinner ____13____ the Huang's. After dinner, they played with their little dog ____14____ back of the house. After that, they began to do their homework. Helen did not un 15____ her homework, so David helped her.

11. _____

12. _____

13. _____

14. _____

15. _____

17 ［第三冊］ 第 9 課

時間：20分鐘 ✽ 得分： ／15分

A 請仔細閱讀下面文章，選出最適當的答案，使句意完整。

A : I can't ___1___ it! It ___2___ . I remember it always rains in Taipei.

B : That's right. But it doesn't usually rain in winter. It usually only rains a lot in spring.

A : I don't like the rain in spring. Spring is a nice season ___3___ . But if there is any rain, we can't go anywhere.

B : What do you think of summer rains?

A : I think it's just wonderful. Sometimes ___4___ in the afternoon, and then it becomes cooler in the evening.

B : But sometimes it rains too much in summer. Taiwan often has ___5___ , which do a lot of damage to the rice crops in· the field.

1. ( ) ① belief　② belief of　③ believe　④ believe of

2. ( ) ① has cleared out　② has cleared on
　　　 ③ has cleared up　④ has cleared down

3. ( ) ① on trips　② for trips　③ on trip　④ for trip

4. ( ) ① there are thundershowers　② there is thundershower
　　　 ③ there are thunder showers④ there is thunder shower

5. ( ) ① tyfoon　② tyfoons　③ typhoon　④ typhoons

B 請仔細閱讀下面文章，將最適當的一個字填入空格中。

It is natural that the weather is different ___6___ place ___7___ place. The weather in northern（北部的）Taiwan often ch_8___ very fast, but the weather in southern（南部的）Taiwan is usually the ___9___ . In Taiwan, it rains a lot in the north, especially in M___10___ and June, and it is sometimes very cold in winter. It does not rain very much in the south, and it is often hot in summer and not very cold in winter there.

6. _____

7. _____

8. _____

9. _____

10. _____

A : I'll go to the market to buy some gl_11___ and a lot of t___12___ . Will you go with me?

B : Yes. But did you h___13___ that? It's thundering. We are going to have much rain. We have to go back before it ___14___ cats and dogs.

A : All right. I have an umbrella ___15___ me and we'll run all the way.

11. _____

12. _____

13. _____

14. _____

15. _____

18 [第三冊] 第**10**課

時間：20分鐘 ＊ 得分： ／10分

A 請仔細閱讀下面文章，選出最適當的答案，使句意完整。

November 12 is a national（國定的）holiday in China. That is the day when Dr. Sun Yat-Sen __1__ . Many people don't have to go to work __2__ that day.

November 12 is also Tom's birthday. Today is November 6. Tom is beginning to plan for a birthday party __3__ .

Tom will clean his apartment on November 11 and his mother will prepare food __4__ his party. His friend, John, will come to his house earlier to help him. The party will start __5__ seven-thirty.

Many of Tom's friends will go to his birthday party. They will all have a lot of fun.

1. (　　) ① borned ② were borned
　　　　 ③ was born ④ was borned

2. (　　) ① in ② on ③ when ④ what

3. (　　) ① last week ② next week
　　　　 ③ three days ago ④ three days later

4. (　　) ① to ② with ③ for ④ in

5. (　　) ① to ② at ③ in ④ on

B 請仔細閱讀下面文章，將最適當的一個字填入空格中。

A : Tomorrow is a holiday, and we won't go to school. What are we going to do?

B : F 6 , we can buy a p 7 t. Tom's birthday party will ____8____ place on Saturday. And then, we can go to the movies.

A : Tom's birthday is tomorrow. I don't un 9 why Tom won't have his party tomorrow.

B : His friends have a lot of time ____10____ the weekend. Some of his friends don't have time tomorrow.

6. _____

7. _____

8. _____

9. _____

10. _____

19 [第三册] 第 **11** 課

時間：20分鐘 ＊ 得分： ／10分

A 請仔細閱讀下面文章，選出最適當的答案，使句意完整。

A : Will you ____1____ come to my home ____2____ New Year's Eve?

B : I'm sorry. I won't stay in Taipei during New Year's. I will visit a friend in Taichung on December 30.

A : I'm sorry. I didn't mean your New Year's Eve. I ____3____ our New Year's Eve. This year's Chinese New Year will come ____4____ the winter vacation.

B : Now I understand. Of course, I will come.

A : The Chinese New Year is a very important holiday. Sons and daughters always go home, and families are together. Everyone is happy and ____5____ during this time. I like it very much.

B : I can't wait!

1. (　　) ① enable ② able ③ able to ④ be able to
2. (　　) ① in ② on ③ at ④ to
3. (　　) ① meaned ② meant ③ mean ④ met
4. (　　) ① at ② on ③ during ④ when
5. (　　) ① had a good time ② have a good time
　　　　 ③ has a good time ④ was a good time

B 請仔細閱讀下面文章，將最適當的一個字填入空格中。

There are many holidays during fall and during winter. Students do not go to school on important holidays. They usually ____6____ holiday's activities before the ____7____ of some holidays.

Confucius' Birthday is ____8____ Day in China. This is because Confucius is regarded（被認為）as the greatest teacher of China.

There are several important holidays in October. Many foreigners（外國人）come to ____9____ Taiwan during this month. However（然而）, the most important holiday in Taiwan is the Chinese New Year. It always comes during the winter ____10____ . Families get together and are very happy on this holiday.

6. _____

7. _____

8. _____

9. _____

10. _____

20 [第三冊] 第 12 課

時間：20分鐘 ＊ 得分： ／15分

A 請仔細閱讀下面文章，選出最適當的答案，使句意完整。

Tom does not like the weather in Taipei. It changes every day in Taipei. Tom ___1___ America, and he ___2___ in New York. The weather in New York is usually the same every day.

This year's winter vacation, Tom is going to visit many places in Taiwan. David and Kevin will go with him. ___3___ by bus on January 26.

They have a lot of plans. They are going to visit a big garden and several beautiful parks. They will also ___4___ Kaohsiung and then buy some gifts there. They will go home ___5___ .

1. (   ) ① came from   ② comes from
          ③ came from the   ④ comes from the
2. (   ) ① was grown up ② grew up ③ grows   ④ grew
3. (   ) ① They will be leaving Taipei
          ② They are leaving Taipei
          ③ They are going leaving Taipei
          ④ They will go leaving Taipei
4. (   ) ① leave   ② leave to ③ leave for ④ leave out
5. (   ) ① before the China New Year Eve
          ② before the China New Year's Eve
          ③ before the Chinese New Year's Eve
          ④ before the Chinese new year's eve

B 請仔細閱讀下面文章，將最適當的一個字填入空格中。

On Teacher's Day, Sue and her
c __6__ went __7__ a picnic in a
scenic spot in the suburbs (郊外) of
Taipei. They invited their teacher to
__8__ them.

It was a f __9__ day, without a
cloud in the sky. They talked, sang,
and played. They all had a good time
with their teacher. When they left, they
carefully put their __10__ into the
__10__ can.

On Christmas Day, Joe and Bill visited some friends together. They talked
with every good friend __11__ the
things that will happen during the vacation. Then __12__ noon, they __13__
lunch at Tom's. __14__ lunch, they
all prayed (祈禱) sincerely (誠懇地) and
hoped for a good tomorrow for the
world. In the evening, they and their
friends had a dance in the school gymnasium (體育館). All the people were
happy. When the dance was over, they
said "so __15__" to each other.

6. _____

7. _____

8. _____

9. _____

10. _____

11. _____

12. _____

13. _____

14. _____

15. _____

21 [第四册] 第 *1* 課

時間：20分鐘 ✻ 得分： ／10分

A 請仔細閱讀下面文章，選出最適當的答案，使句意完整。

Department stores in Taiwan have several restaurants, two or three theaters, and usually a supermarket. ___1___, department stores have sales, and people who want to get bargains（特價品）flock（成群結隊）into the stores. After buying ___2___ they want, they can eat lunch in one of the restaurants. After lunch, they can ___3___. Some people may be interested ___4___ the supermarkets in the basement of the department store. They can buy some food there. In Taipei, many of the big department stores ___5___ small cities.

1. ( ) ① At one time   ② At times
      ③ At all times   ④ In time

2. ( ) ① which   ② thing which   ③ what   ④ that

3. ( ) ① go to movie   ② go to the movies
      ③ go fishing   ④ go to fish

4. ( ) ① in   ② on   ③ by   ④ with

5. ( ) ① like   ② likes   ③ are like   ④ is like

B 請仔細閱讀下面文章，將最適當的一個字填入空格中。

A : ___6___ I help you?

B : Yes, I'd like to see those sweaters there.

A : Here ___7___ are. They are quite cheap.

B : I don't like any of the colors. My daughter's birthday is coming, and I want to buy her a pretty sweater. I suppose (認為) she might prefer a red sweater. Do you have any other colors?

A : Excuse me. There are no ___8___ ones left. We have a branch store (分公司) ___9___ Park Street. Maybe you can buy a red sweater there.

B : O.K. ___10___ you.

6. _____

7. _____

8. _____

9. _____

10. _____

22 [第四冊] 第 2 課

時間：20分鐘 ✻ 得分： ／10分

A 請仔細閱讀下面文章，選出最適當的答案，使句意完整。

Life in a city is quite ____1____ that in the country. In a big city there are many stores; they are bigger and better. On the other hand (另一方面), in the country, there are not many stores and they are usually smaller.

Some people like big cities better than the country because life in a city is very ____2____ . They can always find beautiful clothes in a department store there. The buildings are often more modern. People can go to ____3____ movies and the most important basketball or baseball games there.

Others often visit the country ____4____ the weekend. They like city life during the ____5____ ; but on the week-end they are happier in the country than in a big city.

1. ( )　① similar to　　② different from
　　　　③ different to　　④ similar with
2. ( )　① busy　② noisy　③ convenient　④ bad
3. ( )　① the later　　② the latter
　　　　③ the latest　　④ latest
4. ( )　① when　② on　③ at　　④ when on
5. ( )　① weekend ② Sunday ③ holiday　④ week

B 請仔細閱讀下面文章，將最適當的一個字填入空格中。

Mary lives in Taipei now. Her friend, Tom, lives in the country. Tom is visiting Mary this weekend.

Tom : Mary, we were both b   6   in the country, but now you go to school in Taipei.   7   do you think about life · in a big city?

Mary : You can meet a   8   of friendly people here.

Tom : I don't know. I like the country better. Is city life so wonderful （奇妙的）？

Mary : Not necessarily. Big cities also have their own defects （缺點）.   9   example, the   10   traffic during rush hours （上下班時間） is unpleasant. There are always too many people crowding into the streets, parks, and supermarkets. Sometimes living here makes me uneasy （不安的）.

Tom : Maybe I'm right. Maybe people are happier in the country than in a big city.

6. _____

7. _____

8. _____

9. _____

10. _____

23 [第四册] 第 **3** 課

時間：20分鐘 ＊ 得分： ／10分

A 請仔細閱讀下面文章，選出最適當的答案，使句意完整。

Some people do not use their time well. Sometimes they are very lazy. When they are ___1___ , they are not quick and careful workers. They make many ___2___ . So they usually must do their work several times. They often do their work, but think ___3___ other things at the same time.

One way to succeed is to use your own time well. First, get up early, exercise, and then go to work. At the office you won't want to ___4___ the clock and you will finish your work quickly. Second, proper recreation（娛樂）is good for you. It is necessary（必須的）___5___ you to spend time enjoying some kind of recreation.

1. (　　) ① in the work ② at work
　　　　 ③ at the work ④ in work
2. (　　) ① progresses ② progress
　　　　 ③ mistake ④ mistakes
3. (　　) ① in ② about ③ for ④ with
4. (　　) ① look at ② look into ③ look for ④ look
5. (　　) ① of ② with ③ for ④ to

B 請仔細閱讀下面文章，將最適當的一個字填入空格中。

A： What are your plans ___6___
tomorrow?

B： Well, I have nothing in particular
（特別的） ___7___ do.

A： H__8__ about going for a drive
with me, then?

B： Fine. Where will we ___9___ ?

A： Sun Moon Lake.

B： It always rains in Taipei; maybe it
will be nicer there. What time shall
I come to meet you?

A： Any time after nine is all ___10___ .

B： Shall I come at nine-thirty, then?

A： Yes, that's fine. See you then. Bye.

6. _____

7. _____

8. _____

9. _____

10. _____

24 [第四册] 第 **4** 課

時間：20分鐘 ✻ 得分： ／15分 →

A 請仔細閱讀下面文章，選出最適當的答案，使句意完整。

　　There are many department stores in Taipei. If they have a ___1___ , they are always busier ___2___ usual. Very often a man is not willing to go to the ___3___ Department with his wife, because he is afraid that his wife wants to buy too many things. It is funny, ___4___ it? Maybe ___5___ first, his wife only wants to buy a sweater. But then, after she sees the many beautiful clothes, she is likely to change her mind.

1. (　　) ① business ② guest ③ sale ④ customer
2. (　　) ① at ② than ③ × ④ to
3. (　　) ① Woman's ② Womans' ③ Women's ④ Womens'
4. (　　) ① is ② isn't ③ wasn't ④ won't
5. (　　) ① at ② for ③ in ④ on

B 請仔細閱讀下面文章，將最適當的一個字填入空格中。

I like to live in the country, __6__ there is fresh air, a calm（安靜的）environment, and beautiful scenery. My father is a farmer and he grows rice. Our family makes a __7__ by growing rice. __8__ life in the country is not convenient, it is __9__ quieter. I have three close friends who also live in the country. We often __10__ climbing together. Life in the country is so pleasant（愉快的）. Wouldn't you like to join us?

6. _____

7. _____

8. _____

9. _____

10. _____

When John got home late, his wife looked __11__ him coldly. The children were very sad, because they were not going __12__ a trip to the country. John always seemed to __13__ his promise. He __14__ told his wife and his children __15__ he would take them on a trip in the country. But he told a lie again.

11. _____

12. _____

13. _____

14. _____

15. _____

25 ［第四册］ 第 5 課

時間：20分鐘 ＊ 得分： ／10分

A 請仔細閱讀下面文章，選出最適當的答案，使句意完整。

Having good study habits ___1___ important. In order ___2___ mistakes, when you study, don't think about other things ___3___ the same time. A good desk light is important, too. You will become tired easily ___4___ there is not enough light. Do you like to study in the living room? This is not a good place, because it is usually too ___5___ . You had better study in a quiet place, like your bedroom.

1. ( ) ① are   ② is   ③ do   ④ have
2. ( ) ① to not make   ② to not making
      ③ not to making   ④ not to make
3. ( ) ① at   ② in   ③ on   ④ for
4. ( ) ① when   ② that   ③ if   ④ because
5. ( ) ① noisy   ② noise   ③ voice   ④ voiced

B 請仔細閱讀下面文章，將最適當的一個字填入空格中。

Peter and Bob want to study together this evening, because they are going to have _____6_____ English test tomorrow.

Bob : Tell me, Peter. Where are we going to study?

Peter : Let's study in my bedroom. You can use my brother's desk. He went to his classmate's home to study tonight.

Bob : I like to study _____7_____ the bed.

Peter : That's not a good habit. You won't feel tired so easily _____8_____ you sit at a desk. The light there is better, _____9_____ .

Bob : That's true. My mother a _____10_____ told me to change that habit, but it's not very easy.

Peter : You really need to learn better study habit!

6. _____

7. _____

8. _____

9. _____

10. _____

26 [第四冊] 第 **6** 課

時間：20分鐘 ＊ 得分：　　／10分

A 請仔細閱讀下面文章，選出最適當的答案，使句意完整。

Bob is usually bored with English. He thinks English is not interesting ___1___ . Peter told him that was because he wasn't learning English the correct way.

Bob always studies ___2___ for an English test. Doing this, he has a hard time understanding the English book. He also doesn't know the importance of ___3___ on his own. He never even asks a question when he has ___4___ . So he usually doesn't do very well on an English test.

___5___ , we must learn to think on our own first. This is the key to enjoying learning.

1. (　　) ① at one time ② at all
　　③ in the future ④ for all
2. (　　) ① at the first minute ② at first
　　③ at the last minute ④ at last
3. (　　) ① thinking ② thinks
　　③ thinking about ④ think
4. (　　) ① it ② them ③ some ④ one
5. (　　) ① Enjoying learning ② To enjoy learning
　　③ Enjoyed learning ④ Enjoy learn

B 請仔細閱讀下面文章，將最適當的一個字填入空格中。

Bob : The test in history was really difficult. I didn't ___6___ well.

Peter : I am not surprised by that.

Bob : Why ___7___ ? We studied together all evening.

Peter : Yes, but I usually study a little every evening. You always do a ___8___ of your studying at the last minute.

Bob : I know, but it is not interesting ___9___ me at all.

Peter : History b ___10___ you, because you aren't studying it correctly.

6. _____

7. _____

8. _____

9. _____

10. _____

Our bodies need food to m ___11___ them strong and healthy. Our minds also need a k ___12___ of food. That is knowledge.

To get ___13___ , we must not just remember facts. We have ___14___ understand them! If we can understand all the things that we learn, we will get more knowledge and really enjoy l ___15___ .

11. _____

12. _____

13. _____

14. _____

15. _____

27 [第四冊] 第 7 課

時間：20分鐘 ＊ 得分： ／15分

A 請仔細閱讀下面文章，選出最適當的答案，使句意完整。

Bored people learn things ____1____. If they are not interested in a subject, they usually don't ____2____, thus （因此）they can't make out（了解）their problems. The subject becomes confusing, because they do not try to ____3____ it. Then, a bored person becomes a ____4____ person. In fact, there are no boring or interesting subjects; as long as you ask questions, and learn about a subject ____5____ your own, you will become interested in it.

1. (　　) ① quickly ② slowly ③ quick ④ slow
2. (　　) ① speak ② talk
③ ask questions ④ have problems
3. (　　) ① understand ② find ③ look for ④ reason
4. (　　) ① confusing ② happy ③ sad ④ confused
5. (　　) ① in ② with ③ on ④ for

B 請仔細閱讀下面文章，將最適當的一個字填入空格中。

Henry : Hi, Bob. How about _____6_____
to see the movie, "The Legend
of Sherlock Holmes"？(福爾摩斯
傳奇)

6. _____

Bob : Oh, no. I don't like English
movies. They always speak so
quickly ___7___ I can't follow
them. Besides, I can't go this
evening. I'm going to have tests
___8___ English and m___9___
tomorrow.

7. _____

8. _____

9. _____

10. _____

Henry : Well, if you don't want to go
to the movie with me, I will
see it _____10_____ .

A : Do you know how to _____11_____
pictures with this camera (照相機)？

11. _____

B : No, I don't. I don't know anything
about them at _____12_____ .

12. _____

A : Why ___13___ try to learn how to
use one？You can ask anyone that
knows something about them.

13. _____

14. _____

B : I'll t___14___ your suggestion. Maybe I'll become caught up (被吸引)
_____15_____ photography (攝影術)

15. _____

28 [第四冊] 第 8 課

時間：20分鐘 ＊ 得分： ／15分

A 請仔細閱讀下面文章，選出最適當的答案，使句意完整。

Bob ： Have you finished ＿＿＿1＿＿＿ your homework yet, Peter？

Peter ： I've been writing it ＿＿＿2＿＿＿ , but I haven't finished it yet. After I finish this homework, I will take you to my aunt's. My aunt is a good ＿＿＿3＿＿＿ . If we pay her a visit, we'll be given many delicious things ＿＿＿4＿＿＿ .

Mary ： That sounds good, but I don't want to go to your aunt's, because I am on a diet（節食）.

Bob ： Well, how about going to see a movie？ I know there is an ＿＿＿5＿＿＿ movie at the Star Theater.

Peter ： OK. That's a good idea. I haven't seen a movie in two months.

Mary ： Going to a movie should not make me fat.

1. （ ） ① to write ② writeing ③ writing ④ being written
2. （ ） ① for days ② one day ③ to you ④ for you
3. （ ） ① teacher ② boss ③ cooker ④ cook
4. （ ） ① to be eaten ② to eat ③ for money ④ for nothing
5. （ ） ① excited ② exciting ③ bad ④ beautiful

B 請仔細閱讀下面文章，將最適當的一個字填入空格中。

Tom Brown is my American friend. His hometown is ___6___ Michigan（密西根）, but now he is visiting Taiwan ___7___ his father. L __8__ Sunday, Tom and his father visited my home and stayed with us ___9___ the night. Tom told me that he loves p __10__ computer games because they are exciting. He also told me that he likes Taiwan very much.

6. _____

7. _____

8. _____

9. _____

10. _____

Tom, Joe, and I have different hobbies. Tom likes ___11___ play volleyball （排球）in his free time. Joe loves to swim very ___12___. I think shell （貝殼）co __13__ is the ___14___ interesting. Though we have different ___15___, we are still very good friends.

11. _____

12. _____

13. _____

14. _____

15. _____

29 [第四冊] 第 9 課

時間：20分鐘 ＊ 得分： ／15分

A 請仔細閱讀下面文章，選出最適當的答案，使句意完整。

Tom works in a bookstore. He always puts those expensive books on the highest ___1___ . One day, a big book ___2___ on his foot. His foot was hurt. After Dr. Wang looked at his foot, he gave him a ___3___ of paper ___4___ something on it. Dr. Wang wanted Tom to pay $500, but Tom also wanted Dr. Wang to pay $500 for the book he ___5___ .

1. (　　) ① shelf　　② shelve　　③ shelfs　　④ shelves
2. (　　) ① fall　　② feel　　③ fell　　④ felt
3. (　　) ① peice　　② pecie　　③ piece　　④ piese
4. (　　) ① on　　② to　　③ with　　④ and
5. (　　) ① order　　② ordered　　③ orders　　④ ordering

B 請仔細閱讀下面文章，將最適當的一個字填入空格中。

Tom : Is today your f __6__ t day of
　　　　business？

Clerk : Yes. We will give a discount
　　　　（打折）to every customer（顧客）
　　　　today. __7__ I help you？

Tom : Yes, what's __8__ sale today？

Clerk : You can look at the list（表）
　　　　__9__ the wall. The items
　　　　（項目）of __10__ we sell are
　　　　on it.

Tom : All right. I want to buy these
　　　　boxes of candy.

Clerk : They are all forty dollars. Thank
　　　　you.

6. _____

7. _____

8. _____

9. _____

10. _____

　　Jeff went into a b __11__ to buy
some bread. He bought some b __12__ .
They were two __13__ fifty cents.
Then he bought some co __14__ s,
because the shop was having a special
s __15__ on them.

11. _____

12. _____

13. _____

14. _____

15. _____

30 [第四冊] 第10課

時間：20分鐘 ✻ 得分： ／10分

A 請仔細閱讀下面文章，選出最適當的答案，使句意完整。

Mr. Chen ____1____ a fruit farm in the country. He uses no chemicals on his fruit and grows everything naturally. The fruit that he grows is ____2____ big, but it is sweeter ____3____ healthier than the fruit grown on big farms.

Mr. Chen is making ____4____ money. ____5____ his food is very healthy, nobody wants to spend more money for his fruits. Many farmers use all kinds of chemicals and not all of these chemicals are very safe. Mr. Chen knows it, but most people don't.

1. (　) ① is owned ② owns　③ is belongs ④ belongs to
2. (　) ① not always　　② always not
　　　 ③ no always　　　④ always no
3. (　) ① but　　② or　　③ than　　④ and
4. (　) ① more and more　② much and much
　　　 ③ less and less　　④ little and little
5. (　) ① Although ② Because ③ For　　④ But

B 請仔細閱讀下面文章，將最適當的一個字填入空格中。

Mrs. Benson : _____6_____ comfortable the country is!

Mr. Benson : The country is very nice _____7_____ this time of the year.

Mrs. Benson : Yes, it is, Nature is quite beautiful in fall. And the air is so f____8____ .

Mr. Benson : I've never driven a _____9_____ this road before. Where does it go?

Mrs. Benson : I don't know. This is my first time on it, _____10_____ .

Mrs. Benson : Look o____11____ there. There's a boy walking a____12____ the side of the road. Stop the car.

Mr. Benson : _____13_____ me. Where does this road go to?

Boy : Oh! You are l____14____ . This road goes _____15_____ Taipei.

Mrs. Benson : Thank you. You are so smart.

6. _____

7. _____

8. _____

9. _____

10. _____

11. _____

12. _____

13. _____

14. _____

15. _____

31 [第四冊] 第 11 課

時間：20分鐘 ＊ 得分：　　/10分

A 請仔細閱讀下面文章，選出最適當的答案，使句意完整。

The main streets of my native city are always crowded with（充塞著）cars. It is natural that sometimes there are no ___1___ near my home. Thus, we can see the ___2___ in a mess（混亂）during rush hours（尖峰時間）. To solve （解決）the problem, ___3___ have now taken new steps. They have made some no parking districts（區域）on several roads and don't allow（允許）large vehicles（車輛）to enter the city from 8：00 a.m. to 6：00 p.m. They will also ___4___ the cars that are parked in the wrong places. When the owners find their cars ___5___ , they have to go to the police station to pay the fine. And only then will they be able to drive their cars back.

1. (　) ① parking space　② parking spaces
　　　 ③ park space　④ park spaces
2. (　) ① light　② sign　③ traffic　④ car
3. (　) ① the police　② the teacher
　　　 ③ the drivers　④ the walkers
4. (　) ① take out　② take away
　　　 ③ take apart　④ take into
5. (　) ① run　② go　③ went　④ gone

B 請仔細閱讀下面文章，將最適當的一個字填入空格中。

Tom : Bill, what's wrong with you?
You look very sad.

Bill : I have just had an accident with
my n 6 r's new car. The po-
liceman dealing with the accident
said that I should be responsible
for all of it.

Tom : Why? How did this happen?

Bill : This was the first time I drove
such a new car. I was in such an
excited state that I drove the car
as fast as I could. When I turned
left   7   the traffic light two
blocks away from here, I didn't
notice that the road I drove into
was a one way street. A truck
with a cargo of i 8 t noodles
then slammed into (猛烈撞擊) my
car!

Tom : Maybe t   9   isn't your day.
But you should always be careful
while driving.

Bill : Yes, I should have put on my
g   10   .

6. _____

7. _____

8. _____

9. _____

10. _____

32 [第四冊] 第 **12** 課

時間：20分鐘 ＊ 得分： / 15分

A 請仔細閱讀下面文章，選出最適當的答案，使句意完整。

Natural food has become more and more important in our everyday _____1_____ . Almost all kinds of food have chemicals in them, like fruits, vegetables, instant noodles and so on（等等）. Not many people _____2_____ this before. Most people wanted to buy fruits which were bigger and cheaper, but now they _____3_____ more attention to this problem. They will not choose fruit just _____4_____ its looks because a big and beautiful one doesn't _____5_____ that it will be good for our health.

1. ( )　① lives　　② live　　③ life　　④ lifes
2. ( )　① cared in　　② cared of
　　　　③ cared about　　④ cared out
3. ( )　① take　　② pay　　③ took　　④ paid
4. ( )　① by　　② from　　③ of　　④ in
5. ( )　① means　　② take　　③ takes　　④ mean

B 請仔細閱讀下面文章，將最適當的一個字填入空格中。

Tomorrow is Jane's birthday and we plan to ___6___ a party for her tomorrow night. John and I are preparing all the drinks, fruit, cookies, and bread today. This morning we went to a bakery which was ___7___ opened（新開張的）so we asked the clerk w ___8___ on sale today. He s ___9___ that everything was on special sale. We were so happy that we bought a lot of cookies, buns, and bread there. B ___10___ that we also bought some oranges and tangerines in the supermarket.

6. _____

7. _____

8. _____

9. _____

10. _____

An hour ago, I saw two policemen talking ___11___ front of the restaurant. They b ___12___（帶來）a truck and t ___13___（帶走）all of the cars p ___14___ along the street away, because there's no p ___15___ there.

11. _____

12. _____

13. _____

14. _____

15. _____

33 ［第五册］ 第 **1** 課

時間：20分鐘 ＊ 得分：　　　／15分

A 請仔細閱讀下面文章，選出最適當的答案，使句意完整。

　　　　1　　　your time well is important. People who use their time well are usually healthy and happy. They love to do any activity which can help them　　2　　a strong mind and a healthy body.　　3　　is a popular exercise.

People like running for one reason （理由）　　4　　another. Fat men run to　　5　　weight. Many women run to keep their figures （身材） trim （良好狀況）. To sum up （總而言之）, it is very important for you to use your time well by doing healthful activities.

1. (　　) ① Use 　②Using　③Useing　④Used
2. (　　) ①developed ②developing ③develop ④developt
3. (　　) ① Run　　②Runner　③Running ④Ran
4. (　　) ① and　　②but　　③or　　④to
5. (　　) ① gain　②lose　③lost　④loss

B 請仔細閱讀下面文章，將最適當的一個字填入空格中。

Many people love to know about everything that is h____6____ in the world. The best way to get information（訊息）is to ____7____ newspapers. Of course, ____8____ TV programs is also a good way. You can quickly find ____9____ what is happening or has already happened in the world ____10____ watching TV.

I am good ____11____ controlling and using my time. I get up at dawn（黎明）. I look out of the window, and watch the sun ____12____ . Then I go out ____13____ a walk in the nearby woods. At about 6:30 I go home to eat b____14____ and prepare ____15____ the examination.

6. _____

7. _____

8. _____

9. _____

10. _____

11. _____

12. _____

13. _____

14. _____

15. _____

34 [第五冊] 第 2 課

時間：20分鐘 ＊ 得分： / 15分

A 請仔細閱讀下面文章，選出最適當的答案，使句意完整。

Dear Mary,

Thank you for your letter.

I have an uncle ___1___ Washington. He ___2___ to Japan three times. When he was there, he bought a Japanese camera, and he is very fond of it. He tried to teach me ___3___ to use it, but I can't use it as ___4___ as he.

A few days ago, I visited my uncle, and we went to see the White House. My uncle ___5___ many pictures there with his Japanese camera. I am sending a picture of me taken in front of the White House.

Please send me a picture of yours soon.

I have to say good-bye now.

Your friend,
Tom

1. (　) ① who lives at   ② who live in
       ③ living in   ④ lived
2. (　) ① has gone   ② had gone
       ③ has been going   ④ has been
3. (　) ① which ② how ③ what ④ why
4. (　) ① good ② better ③ well ④ bad
5. (　) ① takes ② makes ③ took ④ made

B 請仔細閱讀下面文章，將最適當的一個字填入空格中。

Our family likes to camp ___6___ the beach ___7___ weekends. We camped there last Sunday. The sun was hot, the sea water ___8___ cool, ___9___ the wind was very strong. We swam a ___10___ day and played in the sand. When I got home, my mother wasn't very happy. "You have brought most of the sand home with you!", she said. Have you ever swum at the beach? Maybe we have swum in the same ocean!

6. _____

7. _____

8. _____

9. _____

10. _____

Last summer Jack and Mary went to the seashore (海濱) ___11___ their mother. Their father was ___12___ busy that he could not go with them. They c__13__ at the beach. At night, they looked ___14___ at the sky. Jack thought ___15___ the moon was like a big round plate (盤子).

11. _____

12. _____

13. _____

14. _____

15. _____

35 [第五冊] 第 3 課

時間：20分鐘 ✻ 得分： ／15分

A 請仔細閱讀下面文章，選出最適當的答案，使句意完整。

Many people are concerned about（關心）the results （結果）of important sport games. When important games are _____1_____ , they often _____2_____ them at work _____3_____ the radio.

_____4_____ do this may even not care about their unfinished （未完成的）work, _____5_____ im-portant it is for them to finish their work. Their team's win-ning becomes the only thing they can care about.

1. ( ) ① play ② plays ③ played ④ playing
2. ( ) ① listening to ② listen to
　　　 ③ listen ④ listened to
3. ( ) ① at ② in ③ on ④ to
4. ( ) ① Who ② Who those ③ Those who ④ Which
5. ( ) ① no matter when ② no matter what
　　　 ③ no matter how ④ no matter which

B 請仔細閱讀下面文章，將最適當的一個字填入空格中。

Baseball is very p___6___ in Taiwan. James likes to play it at school. He also enjoys ___7___ baseball games ___8___ TV. Like most people, he is i___9___ in watching his favorite team to beat the other team. If his favorite team w___10___, he becomes very excited. If it loses, he still likes to watch the game.

6. _____

7. _____

8. _____

9. _____

10. _____

The b___11___ of the company, Tom, likes baseball very much. He has a TV set put in his office in ___12___ to watch the baseball game on TV. Yesterday when the game started, the owner allowed the employees (職員) of the company to s___13___p their work and sit in ___14___ of the TV to watch the game together. They all spent an ex___15___ afternoon.

11. _____

12. _____

13. _____

14. _____

15. _____

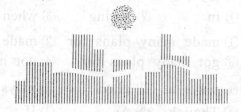

36 **[第五冊]** 第 **4** 課

時間：20分鐘 ✻ 得分： / 15分

A 請仔細閱讀下面文章，選出最適當的答案，使句意完整。

All kinds of activities ____1____ by students when they have free time. Many students have a lot of spare time （閒暇時間）____2____ summer vacation. Two students, Jim and Joe, have already ____3____ their summer vacation.

Jim is a very good soccer player. He ____4____ his school's soccer team. The team has won many games. This summer, he is going to practice soccer every morning. Joe has written to some of his friends. ____5____ the weather is good, they plan to camp in the country or on the beach.

1. ( ) ① are enjoyed   ② are enjoying
　　　 ③ enjoy   ④ have enjoyed
2. ( ) ① in   ② during   ③ when   ④ at
3. ( ) ① made many plans for ② made many plans in
　　　 ③ got many plans for ④ got many plans in
4. ( ) ① plays as ② plays for ③ plays on ④ plays at
5. ( ) ① Though ② As ③ If ④ Whether

B 請仔細閱讀下面文章，將最適當的一個字填入空格中。

Do you like to climb mountains？My friend, Ted ___6___. He began to climb some high hills（小山丘）w___7___ he was still a small boy. Now Ted wants to go to India to climb some of the very high mountains in the Himalayas（喜瑪拉雅山）, b___8___ he is still young ___9___ hasn't got e___10___ money.

6. _____

7. _____

8. _____

9. _____

10. _____

Mark has an American pen pal who will visit him this summer. His pen pal will stay in Taiwan ___11___ two weeks. Mark will ___12___ him ___13___ many famous（有名的）places in Taiwan, such ___14___ Sun Moon Lake and the National Palace Museum（故宮博物院）. Several ___15___ Mark's friends will go with them. Mark has never visited some of these places but his friends have.

11. _____

12. _____

13. _____

14. _____

15. _____

37 [第五册] 第 5 課

時間：20分鐘 ＊ 得分：　　／15分

A 請仔細閱讀下面文章，選出最適當的答案，使句意完整。

Paul is a boy full ___1___ imagination（想像力）and he is good at ___2___ stories. He has made up his mind to become a writer in the future. One day he made a big mistake. He ___3___ a new idea and called the police officer, "The hotel ___4___ my house is ___5___ fire !" When the officers came a few minutes later and asked "Where is the fire ?" Paul said, "What I said was not true. It was only my imagination." This got the officers very angry.

1. (　) ① with　②from　③in　④of

2. (　) ① make up　②make with
　　　③making with　④making up

3. (　) ① think　②thought
　　　③thought of　④think of

4. (　) ① next　②next to　③next from　④next with

5. (　) ① on　②in　③with　④from

B 請仔細閱讀下面文章，將最適當的一個字填入空格中。

One day when I was almost home from school, I ___6___ across a heavy rain. All my dress and shoes（鞋子）became dirty and wet. Mother looked ___7___ me and said, "Oh, baby, hurry i___8___ the bathroom. T___9___ a hot bath right away or you'll c___10___ a cold. I'll bring you some towels and clean clothes." My mother is the best mother in the world and she loves me so much.

6. _____

7. _____

8. _____

9. _____

10. _____

The cage（獸籠）a tiger was in was so strong that he could not ___11___ out of it. He asked an old man ___12___ open the cage. When the old man opened it, the tiger said that he w___13___ eat the man. A dog came and ___14___ the story. The dog asked the tiger to show him how to get into the cage. So the tiger went into the cage. The dog closed the door ___15___ once and saved the old man.

11. _____

12. _____

13. _____

14. _____

15. _____

38 [第五冊] 第 **6** 課

時間：20分鐘 ＊ 得分：　　／15分

A 請仔細閱讀下面文章，選出最適當的答案，使句意完整。

My brother and I dug some big holes to plant some new trees in our garden this afternoon. "＿＿1＿＿ should be a sign or some lights," he said. "These holes aren't safe, and someone might ＿＿2＿＿." I said "Who will walk through our garden?" After ＿＿3＿＿ that, we heard Bob, our neighbor, calling "＿＿4＿＿ the thief and catch him! He is now running into your garden." We ran after the thief but he just ＿＿5＿＿ the big hole. My brother said to me "You're right. There shouldn't be a sign or some lights near these holes."

1. (　　) ① It　　② There　　③ That　　④ This
2. (　　) ① get hurt　　　　② get hurts
　　　　 ③ make hurt　　　 ④ make hurts
3. (　　) ① said　　　　　② say
　　　　 ③ saying　　　　 ④ been saying
4. (　　) ① Stop　② Stopping　③ Stoping　④ Stopped
5. (　　) ① fall into　② fell into　③ fill into　④ feel into

B 請仔細閱讀下面文章，將最適當的一個字填入空格中。

Betty is very happy because she will ___6___ to a camp tomorrow. "Would you like to go together with me?", she asked her sister, Mary. Mary said "That's wonderful. ___7___ like to." Betty wants to borrow ___8___ Mary a backpack, an umbrella, and a swimsuit. This really got Mary ___9___ trouble and she said, "I've le ___10___ you everything that I own and now how can I go together with you?"

6. _____

7. _____

8. _____

9. _____

10. _____

A : Do you have ___11___ brother?

B : Yes, I have a y ___12___ brother.

A : Is he ___13___ enough to go to school?

B : No, he is too young ___14___ go to school.

A : How old is he?

B : He is only ___15___ year old.

11. _____

12. _____

13. _____

14. _____

15. _____

39 [第五冊] 第 7 課

時間：20分鐘 ＊ 得分： ／15分

A 請仔細閱讀下面文章，選出最適當的答案，使句意完整。

One beautiful fall evening, Jack and his classmate, Bob, were walking through a park. They were ___1___ their way to the library. They ___2___ a rest under an old tree in the park. Jack found that there was a wallet (皮夾) with much money ___3___ it. He said "Someone must have lost it. I should take it to the police office." "If I ___4___ you, I would wait here because he must come back to ___5___ his wallet." What would you do if you were Jack ?

1. (　　) ① from　　② of　　③ on　　④ with
2. (　　) ① take　　② took　　③ taking　　④ taken
3. (　　) ① in　　② on　　③ at　　④ of
4. (　　) ① am　　② are　　③ was　　④ were
5. (　　) ① look after　② look upon　③ look for　④ look at

B 請仔細閱讀下面文章，將最適當的一個字填入空格中。

Jack and Bob waited under the old tree in the park for a __6__ (一會兒). There was a man looking really angry and worried __7__ something. "Someone must have stolen my wallet. __8__ can I do now?", he said. They asked him, "Are you looking __9__ your wallet? Is this yours?" "Yes, how did you find it? I used my flashlight and looked for it everywhere. I would have gotten in trouble if I l __10__ it. You really are honest boys. Thank you very much."

6. _____

7. _____

8. _____

9. _____

10. _____

This letter was written to Ken by Rose. Rose was very sorry that her l __11__ was not in time for Christmas. Rose thanked Ken and his family for the good time she __12__ with them. Rose was also so pleased with the beautiful china __13__ to her by Ken's mother __14__ she showed it to her classmates and told them about __15__ history. Rose hopes that Ken will come to her city.

11. _____

12. _____

13. _____

14. _____

15. _____

40 [第五冊] 第 **8** 課

時間：20分鐘 ✻ 得分： ／15分

A 請仔細閱讀下面文章，選出最適當的答案，使句意完整。

I went to a soccer game with my father last night. The game was so violent (激烈的) ____1____ the spectators (觀眾) ____2____ their breath as the two teams tried to ____3____ the tie in the last minute of the game.

"The red team seems to be running ____4____ of energy (精力)." I asked my father, "Do you think they will lose the game?"

"My dear son," he answered, "____5____ would be better if you just watched more and talked less."

I was not very happy at that time. Was I wrong?

1. (　) ① that　　② it　　③ this　　④ these
2. (　) ① held　　② hold　　③ take　　④ took
3. (　) ① give　　② break　　③ make　　④ put
4. (　) ① in　　② into　　③ out　　④ up
5. (　) ① that　　② this　　③ these　　④ it

B 請仔細閱讀下面文章，將最適當的一個字填入空格中。

My birthday will come next Wednesday. My father wants to buy ___6___ a birthday present. He asked me, "What do you like best, a sweater, a jacket or a dictionary?" I do need an English dictionary so I chose a dictionary ___7___ my present. W 8 do you think I want a dictionary? To tell the truth, if I ___9___ a dictionary ___10___ my own, I will not make any more mistakes in the letter to my girl friend.

6. _____

7. _____

8. _____

9. _____

10. _____

One day, Tom and his brother Peter ___11___ fishing by the riverside. They waited for the fish to come. Unfortunately, the fish weren't b 12 . Peter went home. But Tom waited for the big fish. Still, no fish. But then just as he was about to give ___13___, he had a good idea. He hurried over to the fish store.

"What can I do ___14___ you, boy?" asked the owner of the store.

"I want the ___15___ fish you have," answered Tom.

11. _____

12. _____

13. _____

14. _____

15. _____

41 [第五冊] 第 **9** 課
時間：20分鐘 ✱ 得分： / 15分

A 請仔細閱讀下面文章，選出最適當的答案，使句意完整。

John and Mary are good friends. They took a walk in a beautiful park the day before yesterday. While they were walking ___1___ the pond, something ___2___ their eyes. They saw some trash there. "I am ___3___ and sad to see this," John said. "Why do people throw trash on the ground and don't care ___4___ the cleanliness of the park?"

"It is better to do than to ___5___." Upon saying that, Mary picked up the trash and threw it in the trash can.

1. ( ) ① of ② along ③ at ④ in
2. ( ) ① catch ② get ③ got ④ caught
3. ( ) ① surprised ② surprise
　　　 ③ surprising ④ be surprised
4. ( ) ① to ② about ③ of ④ after
5. ( ) ① ask ② speak ③ complain ④ need

B 請仔細閱讀下面文章，將最適當的一個字填入空格中。

Judy and Sarah talked ____6____ music on their way home from school. Judy said that she likes to listen to rock music and she can ____7____ the guitar. Sarah said that she can only play the drums. Suddenly, a boy called loudly f __8__ their back, "Would you please ____9____ me a hand?" The box he carried looked heavy.

6. _____

7. _____

8. _____

9. _____

10. _____

"This box is full of rock records. I borrowed it from my friend to listen to them." Judy was happy to hear that and suggested, "Can we listen to them with you?" "Why not? T __10__ a good idea!", the boy replied.

When I was ____11____ home from school, I found a little dog. It had no home. The dog was so weak (虛弱) ____12____ I felt very sorry for it and took it home. My family liked the dog. It has ____13____ one of my family now. I take care ____14____ him every day. He likes living with ____15____ .

11. _____

12. _____

13. _____

14. _____

15. _____

42 [第五册] 第 **10** 課

時間：20分鐘 ＊ 得分：　　／15分

A 請仔細閱讀下面文章，選出最適當的答案，使句意完整。

One day, a hunter set a net in the forest, and a lion got caught in it. The lion could not understand how this could happen because he was usually very ____1____ . The great animal was in great ____2____ . Loud, angry noises could ____3____ everywhere in the forest. As soon as the mouse heard these noises, he went to see ____4____ was wrong. Finding the lion in the net, the small mouse started to bite the net. Soon little pieces of the net fell to the ground. One piece then, another piece fell … and another. ____5____ a short time, the lion was free again.

1. (　　) ① happy 　② careful 　③ angry 　④ careless
2. (　　) ① crazy 　② angry 　③ happy 　④ trouble
3. (　　) ① hear 　　　　　② be heard
　　　　③ have been heard 　④ have heard
4. (　　) ① what 　② how 　③ that 　④ which
5. (　　) ① After 　② Before 　③ Such 　④ So

B 請仔細閱讀下面文章，將最適當的一個字填入空格中。

It is ___6___ that there once was a man called Aesop, ___7___ told many fables more than two thousand years ___8___ . Today these fables are called Aesop's Fables. Fables are stories that teach us the difference ___9___ right and wrong. And these stories tell us how to get ___10___ with other people.

6. _____

7. _____

8. _____

9. _____

10. _____

Judy : Sue, someone is r__11____ the bell. Would you see who it is?

Sue : It must be Paul.

Sue goes to o__12____ the door.

Paul : Hi, Sue. I hope I'm not late.

Sue : You are early. It's so kind ___13___ you to come here. I was worried that no one would help me fix my tape recorder. Would you do me a ___14___ ?

Paul : All right. I'll repair it at ___15___ .

11. _____

12. _____

13. _____

14. _____

15. _____

43 [第五冊] 第 11 課

時間：20分鐘 ＊ 得分： ／15分

A 請仔細閱讀下面文章，選出最適當的答案，使句意完整。

When it comes to（每當提及）the great ___1___ of ancient（古老的）China, people often think of Confucius and Chuang-tzu. They had ___2___ thoughts not only on politics ___3___ on the idea of nature. Chuang-tzu, for example, thought people should live with nature and be subject to it（服從它）. And he thought that people did not need a government（政府）at all. However, Confucius insisted（強調）that a government was necessary and people had the ___4___ to change their bad surroundings. When facing trouble, one should by no means（絕不）give ___5___ .

1. (　　) ① speakers　　　② thinkers
　　　　　③ hunters　　　④ politicians

2. (　　) ① the same　　　② like
　　　　　③ different　　　④ likely

3. (　　) ① but　　② and　　③ or　　④ otherwise

4. (　　) ① able　　② happy　　③ need　　④ ability

5. (　　) ① up　　② out　　③ away　　④ forth

B 請仔細閱讀下面文章，將最適當的一個字填入空格中。

Paul : Would you mind if I watch you practice today?

Judy : ___6___ course not. But we might not be able to practice today. There is something ___7___ with my guitar. Paul, s__8__ you study electronics, could you look at it?

Paul : I don't need to look at it. I already know ___9___ the trouble is. There is no electricity today ___10___ eight to twelve.

In Great Britain (英國) people drive cars to the left and so do those in Japan. Stop and look both ways when c__11__ the street. In Great Britain, you must look r__12__ first, then look ___13___, and look ___14___ again. When the road is c__15__, then you may cross it.

6. _____

7. _____

8. _____

9. _____

10. _____

11. _____

12. _____

13. _____

14. _____

15. _____

44 [第五冊] 第 12 課

時間：20分鐘 ✻ 得分：　　/ 15分

A 請仔細閱讀下面文章，選出最適當的答案，使句意完整。

I am really glad to have two American neighbors, Judy and Sarah. We have the same interests. Their rock band is going to make their first ＿＿＿1＿＿＿ next month. All of the songs were written ＿＿＿2＿＿＿ Judy and Sarah. Today they tried to write a song about China, but they didn't understand China at all, so they ＿＿＿3＿＿＿ me to help them. I told them about the Chinese fable of the old man who wanted to move a mountain.

I almost couldn't believe it! They wrote an English song about the fable right away, the name of which is "The Man ＿＿＿4＿＿＿ Could Move Mountains," and then we ＿＿＿5＿＿＿ it together.

1. (　　) ① book ② record ③ newspaper ④ magazine
2. (　　) ① in ② with ③ by ④ to
3. (　　) ① wake ② ask ③ tell ④ asked
4. (　　) ① who ② whose ③ Whose ④ Who
5. (　　) ① sung ② sang ③ sing ④ song

B 請仔細閱讀下面文章，將最適當的一個字填入空格中。

Mr. March : ___6___ are you doing, Ken?

Ken : I'm reading a book.

Mr. March : What book are your reading?

Ken : ___7___ old Chinese story.

Mr. March : Do you like old stories?

Ken : Yes, b__8__ I read many other kinds of books. too.

Mr. March : You are fond ___9___ reading, aren't you?

Ken : ___10___, I am. And my sister likes it very much also.

6. _____

7. _____

8. _____

9. _____

10. _____

Judy and Sarah ___11___ very surprised that I could sing. I told them that I learned ___12___ to sing well when I was young. I also told them that I sang ___13___ a children's TV program many years ago. Today, they wanted me to sing a song they have written. I was glad ___14___ have had the opportunity to be a ___15___ .

11. _____

12. _____

13. _____

14. _____

15. _____

45 [第六册] 第 7 課

時間：20分鐘 ＊ 得分：　　/15分

A 請仔細閱讀下面文章，選出最適當的答案，使句意完整。

The China Youth Corps ___1___ many activities during summer and winter vacations. These activities are very ___2___ among our students. Through these programs, the CYC can help to ___3___ character in our youths and make their bodies stronger.

In summer, to go ___4___ in the mountains is very helpful to our health. Swimming is also wonderful. It can make us feel cooler. In winter, if you have never seen snow, you can go ___5___ with the CYC's teachers. It is safe and exciting.

1. (　) ① hold 　 ② holds 　 ③ happen 　 ④ happens
2. (　) ① popular 　　　　 ② populared
　　　　 ③ populous 　　　　 ④ populate
3. (　) ① make 　 ② build 　 ③ do 　 ④ get
4. (　) ① swimming 　　　　 ② fishing
　　　　 ③ sweeping 　　　　 ④ hiking
5. (　) ① sking 　 ② skiing 　 ③ skying 　 ④ skateing

B 請仔細閱讀下面文章，將最適當的一個字填入空格中。

Many people, es ___6___ girls, are afraid ___7___ cockroaches. That seems to be very interesting, because cockroaches are very small. Allen even uses r ___8___ bands to kill them. He calls it his "night hunting w ___9___ a gun." Of course, he didn't s ___10___ that night.

6. _____

7. _____

8. _____

9. _____

10. _____

It is great fun to go c ___11___ in the woods. J ___12___ in this activity, you may learn ___13___ to start a f ___14___ without matches. You may also learn the way to cook meals outdoors (戶外). But if there is a t ___15___ n, such an activity may be dangerous and so it may not be held.

11. _____

12. _____

13. _____

14. _____

15. _____

46 ［第六冊］ 第 **2** 課

時間：20分鐘 ✱ 得分：　　 /15分

A 請仔細閱讀下面文章，選出最適當的答案，使句意完整。

Hard work ____1____ boys become men. Rick was a
very stupid boy before. He was
afraid to express（表達）himself,
but he is not ____2____ he used
to be. He found a job in a
fishing company. He ____3____
to get up very early to deal
____4____ cargoes（貨物）. It
was a very hard job, but it was
also a good opportunity（機會）
for him to learn how to get
along ____5____ people.

1. (　　) ① make 　　② makes 　　③ made 　　④ maid
2. (　　) ① like 　　② as 　　③ what 　　④ that
3. (　　) ① was 　　② has 　　③ have 　　④ had
4. (　　) ① by 　　② with 　　③ without 　　④ upon
5. (　　) ① for 　　② by 　　③ with 　　④ of

B 請仔細閱讀下面文章，將最適當的一個字填入空格中。

After g　6　 from senior high school, Jack decided to be a sailor （水手）. Before he became a qualified （合格的） sailor, he had to have a c 7 p. The doctor checked his b 8 y first. Second, he checked his e 9 rs and eyes. Because Jack was very h 10 y, he passed the check quickly.

6. _____

7. _____

8. _____

9. _____

10. _____

I like the sea. Sometimes I feel like a small boat t 11 floats at sea. I g 12 up in the port of Keelung. When I was a small child, I usually ___13___ fishing with my father. B 14 I liked fish, I often told the fish to run ___15___ when my father tried to catch them.

11. _____

12. _____

13. _____

14. _____

15. _____

47 [第六冊] 第 **3** 課

時間：20分鐘 ＊得分：____／15分

A 請仔細閱讀下面文章，選出最適當的答案，使句意完整。

I ___1___ this small room with my classmate, Betty. Before we moved into it, it was so dirty ___2___ we had to clean it. Now we have finally made our apartment ___3___ more comfortable. Betty and I painted the walls yellow, so our place seems warmer in winter. We changed all of the screens, so there are fewer ___4___ in summer. We also raise a cat now. Her name is Spot, and she kills ___5___ every day.

1. ( ) ① give ② stay ③ live in ④ have
2. ( ) ① that ② but ③ and that ④ when
3. ( ) ① looked ② looks ③ looking ④ look
4. ( ) ① moskitos ② moskitoes
   ③ mosquitoes ④ mosguitoes
5. ( ) ① animals ② dogs ③ persons ④ roaches

B 請仔細閱讀下面文章，將最適當的一個字填入空格中。

____6____ summer nights, I usually hear the sound of many grasshoppers（蚱蜢）. The sound is ____7____ a melody（旋律）. Listening ____8____ their sound is pleasant. In summer, mosquitoes are a nuisance（令人討厭的東西）. They keep on ____9____ me, and it makes me ____10____ crazy.

6.＿＿＿＿＿

7.＿＿＿＿＿

8.＿＿＿＿＿

9.＿＿＿＿＿

10.＿＿＿＿＿

It s__11__ that no one ____12____ a good time at the party last night. The music s__13__ too classical（古典的）and the living room was too small. The dishes were not d__14__s at all. The chicken t__15__ like overdone（太焦的）beef steak. To sum up（總之）, nothing was good.

11.＿＿＿＿＿

12.＿＿＿＿＿

13.＿＿＿＿＿

14.＿＿＿＿＿

15.＿＿＿＿＿

48 [第六册] 第 **4** 課

時間：20分鐘 ✻ 得分：　　／15分

A 請仔細閱讀下面文章，選出最適當的答案，使句意完整。

Summer vacation was in July. Tom and Mary wanted to ____1____ traveling. First they went to Suao on their own, ____2____ their friend, Rick Wang. Rick Wang ____3____ the two Americans his new boat, and then they went to watch the sunrise (日出). Later they went fishing. This was Tom's first time on a boat, so he became uncomfortable and ____4____. He could only sit there and ____5____ the other two fishing.

1. (　) ① be 　　② take 　　③ make 　　④ go

2. (　) ① to visit 　　　　　② visiting
　　　　 ③ and visit 　　　　④ and visiting

3. (　) ① gave 　② showed 　③ told 　④ said

4. (　) ① hungry 　② sad 　③ happy 　④ afraid

5. (　) ① take 　② like 　③ watch 　④ make

B 請仔細閱讀下面文章，將最適當的一個字填入空格中。

It was a very hot afternoon. Tom went fishing ___6___ John. They caught a bus going to Suao ___7___ three p.m. Tom c 8 thirteen fish, ___9___ John only got one little fish. After three hours, they went home to cook the fish ___10___ dinner.

6. _____

7. _____

8. _____

9. _____

10. _____

Allen, Jack, and Rick were camping b 11 the river. Allen helped Rick s 12 a fire and grill the fish. Jack changed his clothes and sat near the fire, but he didn't look very happy. "What's w 13 ?" asked Allen.

"Another mosquito bit me."

Jack f 14 very sick and want to rest. He finally h 15 a quiet vacation in the hospital !

11. _____

12. _____

13. _____

14. _____

15. _____

49 [第六冊] 第 5 課

時間：20分鐘 ＊ 得分： ／15分

A 請仔細閱讀下面文章，選出最適當的答案，使句意完整。

Many years ago in America, people went shopping
___1___ different stores. The housewife（家庭主婦）bought
meat and vegetables in one store, but bought bread in
___2___ . It was very troublesome（麻煩的；討厭的）and

they had to ___3___ a lot of
time shopping. Going shopping
is more convenient today. There
are supermarkets ___4___ .
People can buy ___5___ at
one time.

1. (　　) ① in ② of ③ by ④ at
2. (　　) ① another ② the other ③ others ④ the others
3. (　　) ① take ② spend ③ cost ④ have
4. (　　) ① selling not only food but also every other thing
② not only selling food but every other thing
③ selling food not only but also everything
④ selling not food but everything
5. (　　) ① all them ② them all
③ all of they ④ they all

B 請仔細閱讀下面文章，將最適當的一個字填入空格中。

Many people do not enjoy going shopping or deciding ___6___ to buy. They prefer ___7___ eat at a fast-food restaurant. Such a person might look at the m___8___ and say, "I'd ___9___ a large hamburger, french fries, and a cola." And the clerk might ___10___, "What size of cola, sir? Small, medium, or large?"

6. _____
7. _____
8. _____
9. _____
10. _____

Rachel : This shopping center is s___11___ large. ___12___ is that paint store? I thought you knew.

Jill : I thought it was right here. I'm getting a ___13___ confused. This is the third time we've gone ___14___ this ice cream shop.

Rachel : I think you ___15___ be mixed up.

11. _____
12. _____
13. _____
14. _____
15. _____

50 [第六冊] 第 **6** 課

時間：20分鐘 ✻ 得分： / 15分

A 請仔細閱讀下面文章，選出最適當的答案，使句意完整。

Today environmental（環境的）pollution is getting worse and worse. So there are many countries ___1___ laws to fight pollution. Factories now must clean their waste water ___2___ it is thrown away. They also cannot blow dirty smoke into the air.

More and more cars are now using gas ___3___ lead（鉛）in it. Many things need to be done, however. We can all help. We can use paper bags, not ___4___ ones. We can put trash in the trash ___5___, instead of（而不要）throwing it on the ground.

1. (　) ① make ② making
   ③ who make ④ to make
2. (　) ① after ② when ③ before ④ as
3. (　) ① having ② with ③ without ④ no
・4. (　) ① rock ② good ③ plastic ④ stone
5. (　) ① bottle ② can ③ vessel ④ bag

B 請仔細閱讀下面文章，將最適當的一個字填入空格中。

Hundreds of years ago, people did not have modern co __6__ s like air-planes. Life today has new p __7__ , such as pollution. There are water pollution, n __8__ pollution and many other kinds of pollution. Air pollution is the most s __9__ kind of pollution. When air is very thick with pollutants（污染物）we call it smog. We must make laws to f __10__ pollution.

6. ＿＿＿＿＿

7. ＿＿＿＿＿

8. ＿＿＿＿＿

9. ＿＿＿＿＿

10. ＿＿＿＿＿

Clerk : May I help you?

Jill : Yes. We'd like to buy some paint and twelve big paint-brushes.

Clerk : Are you sure you n __11__ so many brushes?

Jill : Yes, because we are going to ＿＿__12__＿＿ a painting party.

Clerk : A painting party?

Jill : That's right. Our apartment is so big ＿＿__13__＿＿ we can't paint it by o __14__ . Our classmates will h __15__ us.

11. ＿＿＿＿＿

12. ＿＿＿＿＿

13. ＿＿＿＿＿

14. ＿＿＿＿＿

15. ＿＿＿＿＿

51 [第六册] 第 **7** 課

時間：20分鐘 ＊ 得分： ／15分

A 請仔細閱讀下面文章，選出最適當的答案，使句意完整。

It is natural that people dream ____1____ the future, but not everyone ____2____ more than dream. Whether a man can make his dreams ____3____ partly depends on his strong will（意志）. ____4____ , he must be able to face（面對）failure.

I once dreamed ____5____ a city for my family, but now I find it impractical（不合實際的）. After all, one should have dreams that are more practical.

1. (　) ① at ② to ③ about ④ on
2. (　) ① do ② did ③ does ④ is
3. (　) ① come to true ② come in true
　　　 ③ come true ④ come of true
4. (　) ① At the time ② At the same time
　　　 ③ At times ④ At that time
5. (　) ① to build ② of building
　　　 ③ to build of ④ of building up

B 請仔細閱讀下面文章，將最適當的一個字填入空格中。

Walt Disney is a man ___6___ name is known all over the world. He had his dreams come true. ___7___ his dream city, people go shopping by electric cars and buses. In that world, trains are quiet and m ___8___ no noise. Doors open ___9___ themselves and are controlled by computers. All seems like m ___10___ !

6. _____

7. _____

8. _____

9. _____

10. _____

Paul : Of course, I remember. But I don't know ___11___ I can go or not.

Jill : Why not?

Paul : Today wasn't my ___12___ . There was a thundershower this afternoon, and I didn't have an umbrella ___13___ me. As ___14___ as I got home, I took ___15___ my wet clothes, and dried my hair. But I think I am catching a cold.

11. _____

12. _____

13. _____

14. _____

15. _____

52 [第六冊] 第 8 課

時間：20分鐘 ＊ 得分： ／15分

A 請仔細閱讀下面文章，選出最適當的答案，使句意完整。

For some people, it is a waste of time to _____1_____ too long on eating. Maybe it is because they don't like cooking. A good way for these people to eat is fast food. Fast food is _____2_____ like the name says : it is food served fast, and can be _____3_____ fast. The most _____4_____ fast foods are hamburgers (漢堡) and french fries (薯條). Fast food can _____5_____ you a lot of time.

1. (　) ① used 　　② spent 　　③ spend 　　④ using
2. (　) ① just 　　② in 　　③ eaten 　　④ enjoyed
3. (　) ① take 　　② eating 　　③ took 　　④ eaten
4. (　) ① enjoys 　　② like 　　③ best 　　④ popular
5. (　) ① make 　　② save 　　③ spent 　　④ buys

B 請仔細閱讀下面文章，將最適當的一個字填入空格中。

Fast food is designed (設計) to save the c　6　 more time, but often people w　7　 too much time in ordering (點) it. If you waste time ordering the food you may waste more time ___8___ you save! Therefore it is very important not ___9___ to make the right decision (決定), but ___10___ not to spend too long on it.

6. _____

7. _____

8. _____

9. _____

10. _____

Robert：Let's ___11___ to eat something.

Jennifer：Where do you ___12___ to go?

Robert：How about a fast food restaurant? It's c　13　, cheap, and I haven't had a hamburger for a ___14___ time.

Jennifer：Sure. I'd ___15___ to go.

11. _____

12. _____

13. _____

14. _____

15. _____

53 [第六冊] 第 **9** 課

時間：20分鐘 ＊ 得分： ／15分

A 請仔細閱讀下面文章，選出最適當的答案，使句意完整。

Everyone and ＿＿＿1＿＿＿ has a name. All names have a meaning and a story behind where it came from, but it is ＿＿2＿＿ how little we know about our own names.

Apart from old names, there are always new names being ＿＿3＿＿ . For example, products such as the walkman（隨身聽）. ＿＿＿4＿＿＿ a new name given to a product, the personal（個人）stereo（音響）, but now we ＿＿5＿＿ as a general name for all personal stereos.

1. ( ) ① all ② everything
   ③ every people ④ all people
2. ( ) ① known ② wrong ③ surprising ④ interests
3. ( ) ① invented ② make up ③ come up ④ create
4. ( ) ① This ② It was ③ Be ④ Before
5. ( ) ① use it ② think ③ used ④ have

B 請仔細閱讀下面文章，將最適當的一個字填入空格中。

Names are very u __6__ l in our
lives. They can be as important as the
things they mean. When names are
__7__ up they have a certain meaning,
but after a w __8__ people forget the
__9__ , and so the name loses its
meaning. It __10__ meaningless.

6. _____

7. _____

8. _____

9. _____

10. _____

Lewis : Have you ever __11__
about what your name means?

Margaret : I know my name is from
Latin（拉丁文）and means
"pearl"（珍珠）. What about
your name?

Lewis : Well, it means "famous
in war." In the past it
__12__ probably given
only to those who won in the
battle. My name might be
__13__ old as some of the
ancient（古代的）b __14__ !
But now w __15__ you are
famous in war or not, you
can be called "Lewis."

11. _____

12. _____

13. _____

14. _____

15. _____

54 [第六冊] 第10課

時間：20分鐘 ＊ 得分：　　/15分

A 請仔細閱讀下面文章，選出最適當的答案，使句意完整。

How words come ____1____ can be very interesting. When the first Germans went to America, they cooked round（圓的）____2____ of beef（牛肉）. The Americans asked what those pieces of beef were called, but the Germans ____3____ the Americans were asking ____4____ they came from, so they answered : Hamburg. And to this day, the Americans ____5____ call those round pieces of beef "hamburgers"（漢堡）.

1. (　　) ① from ② in ③ out ④ down
2. (　　) ① blocks ② pieces ③ meats ④ pies
3. (　　) ① believing ② knows ③ think ④ thought
4. (　　) ① where ② how ③ when ④ whenever
5. (　　) ① wants to ② to ③ still ④ Germans

B 請仔細閱讀下面文章，將最適當的一個字填入空格中。

There are many ____6____ languages in this world. And as long as people speak them, the language will live. Each language is different and special in their own ways. Sometimes, ____7____ than making up（造出）new words for something, a language will ____8____ a word from another ____9____. For example, the Americans call the Chinese pan（平底鍋）a "wok", ____10____ that is what it is called in Cantonese.

6. _____

7. _____

8. _____

9. _____

10. _____

Joe : Look! Here are some pictures of me on holiday.

Susan : Yes, these pictures show ____11____ you went to. It's Hawaii（夏威夷）____12____ it?

Joe : Of course. You p__13__y guessed it from the shots （拍攝）of the palm（棕櫚） trees. It's so nice being able to be go on holiday now and t__14__.

Susan : Yes, as long as I h__15__ enough money, I'll go on holiday too!

11. _____

12. _____

13. _____

14. _____

15. _____

55 [第六冊] 第 **11** 課

時間：20分鐘 ＊ 得分： ／15分

A 請仔細閱讀下面文章，選出最適當的答案，使句意完整。

Languages are tools people use to communicate（溝通）with each other and they, like people, live and die. A ____1____ language is a language which people do not use any more. A ____2____ language is the one used by people today, and grows and changes ____3____ time. Some old words ____4____ new meanings, and new words are continuously（不斷地）invented （創造）. Other words may die and only be found in books ____5____ were published（出版）a long time ago.

1. (　) ① death ② die ③ dead ④ died
2. (　) ① life ② living ③ lived ④ live
3. (　) ① with ② to ③ as ④ from
4. (　) ① developed ② found ③ develop ④ are found
5. (　) ① who ② what ③ which ④ when

B 請仔細閱讀下面文章，將最適當的一個字填入空格中。

Languages are always changing. In the ____6____ , it was wrong to say, "He is four years older than me." Today, however, most Americans speak this w 7 . As l 8 as a language lives, it will surely grow and develop. ____9____ is correct or wrong today, may not be so in the f 10 .

6. _____

7. _____

8. _____

9. _____

10. _____

Don : ____11____ do you deliver news-papers?

Ken : It is a good exercise. It m 12 my legs and arms stronger. Throwing newspapers ____13____ good practice. I hope to join the baseball t 14 this summer.

Don : It s 15 a good idea. Can I help you?

Ken : O.K.

11. _____

12. _____

13. _____

14. _____

15. _____

56 [第六冊] 第 **12** 課

時間：20分鐘 ✱ 得分： / 15分 ➡

A 請仔細閱讀下面文章，選出最適當的答案，使句意完整。

Dictionaries are important tools for learning a language. We all have used dictionaries to look ____1____ a new word. In fact, a good dictionary tells us many things, and not just ____2____ a word means. If we see a long, difficult new word in some book, we may consult （查閱） a dictionary, and it will show us ____3____ to use this word. It will also show us ____4____ a word is pronounced.

If we can ____5____ good use of a dictionary, we will make great progress （進步） in our language learning.

1. ( ) ① down ② for ③ up ④ to
2. ( ) ① what ② which ③ how ④ when
3. ( ) ① where ② how ③ what ④ which
4. ( ) ① where ② how ③ what ④ which
5. ( ) ① have ② do ③ make ④ come

B 請仔細閱讀下面文章，將最適當的一個字填入空格中。

Because languages d __6__ p continuously（不斷地）, dictionaries also need to be pr __7__ again every ten years or so in __8__ to show these new changes. Some people are __9__ lazy to consult（查閱）a dictionary. But we should know that dictionaries tell us many interesting facts. After we have learned __10__ to use them, they will become the most important book that we own.

6. _____

7. _____

8. _____

9. _____

10. _____

Today, English is very different __11__ the English spoken long, long ago. __12__ the twelfth century（世紀）, the language had changed so much __13__ people could not read things written in the year 700. Today, we can't understand e __14__ of those forms of English __15__ a special dictionary.

11. _____

12. _____

13. _____

14. _____

15. _____

57 時間：20分鐘 ＊ 得分： ／10分

A 請仔細閱讀下面文章，選出最適當的答案，使句意完整。

Tom goes to a store in New York to buy a present for his brother.

Clerk : Good afternoon. May I help you?

Tom : Yes, please. I want to buy a pen for my brother. Will you ___1___ me some pens?

Clerk : Yes. They're ___2___ there. What color do you want?

Tom : I'd like to get a blue ___3___ .

Clerk : How about this one? It's very popular among students.

Tom : ___4___ .

Clerk : Seventeen dollars.

Tom : Fine. I'll take it. ___5___ twenty dollars.

Clerk : Here's your change. Eighteen, nineteen, and twenty. Thank you very much.

1. ( ) ① want　② take　③ show　④ help
2. ( ) ① in　② over　③ at　④ by
3. ( ) ① one　② pencil　③ ones　④ color
4. ( ) ① How much are they?　② How many is it?
　　　　③ How much is it?　④ How many are they?
5. ( ) ① This is　② Here are　③ It is　④ Here is

B 請仔細閱讀下面文章，將最適當的一個字填入空格中。

Donald （唐老鴨） was ___6___ in the river. He was very happy. ___7___ was a very hot day.

Then Mickey （米老鼠） came up to the river. The cool river looked so good to him ___8___ he wanted to swim, too.

Mickey jumped into the water. But he forgot he couldn't swim at all.

"Help me ! Help !" he cried out.

"Take my hand !" shouted （叫） Donald. "I'll help you." He took Mickey out of the river.

"Thank you, Donald," said Mickey.

"___9___ careful. You must learn ___10___ to swim," said Donald with a smile.

6. _____

7. _____

8. _____

9. _____

10. _____

58 時間：20分鐘 ＊ 得分： ／15分

A 請仔細閱讀下面文章，選出最適當的答案，使句意完整。

With more and more serious environmental（環境的）problems, we must ___1___ an effort to do something about them. The government（政府）should find some ways ___2___ our environment, and the people should do something, too. But ___3___ can we do？For example, if we see someone throwing garbage（垃圾）in the wrong place, we should tell him ___4___ so. We can also set ___5___ a group to protect（保護）our environment. To sum up（總之）, we should play our part to make our life more pleasant（愉快的）.

1. （ ） ① make ② take ③ use ④ try
2. （ ） ① to ② to improve
　　　　③ improve ④ improved
3. （ ） ① how ② where ③ what ④ who
4. （ ） ① not do ② not doing
　　　　③ to do ④ not to do
5. （ ） ① up ② for ③ with ④ at

B 請仔細閱讀下面文章，將最適當的一個字填入空格中。

More Japanese visited the United States in 1986 __6__ Americans visited Japan. This fact made Americans very happy __7__ they have been upset（苦惱）by the trade deficit （貿易赤字）for a long time. __8__ the other hand, the number of European （歐洲的）visitors became larger by 28 percent. This means that more people all __9__ the world now like to go to A __10__ than before.

6. _____

7. _____

8. _____

9. _____

10. _____

Tom likes swimming very much. Last year Tom and his two brothers spent the summer holidays __11__ his aunt's house near the sea. Every day the boys put __12__ their swimming-shorts（泳褲）before breakfast. They spent most __13__ the time in the sea or on the beach till they were tired and hungry. __14__ lunch and supper（晚餐）time, their aunt rang a bell. When the boys heard the bell, they went back to the house __15__ food.

11. _____

12. _____

13. _____

14. _____

15. _____

59

時間：20分鐘 ＊ 得分： ／10分

A 請仔細閱讀下面文章，選出最適當的答案，使句意完整。

All the young students are very glad to hear that the ban on hairstyles (髮禁) has been eliminated (解除). However, class work seems to be ___1___ than hair style.

Beautiful outside looks can let you feel bright (開朗) and ___2___, but "reading" can help you learn, ___3___ is really the best food for the mind. To get better grades and make yourself rich in mind, you have to study harder, ___4___ you?

So, spend ___5___ your time on class work, not on hair.

1. (　) ① very much important ② even much important
   ③ much more important ④ very more important
2. (　) ① happy ② happily ③ sad ④ sadly
3. (　) ① where ② which ③ what ④ that
4. (　) ① don't ② haven't ③ aren't ④ do
5. (　) ① the most of ② most of the
   ③ most the of ④ most of

B 請仔細閱讀下面文章，將最適當的一個字填入空格中。

Tom : Can you sing the Chinese song "Tomorrow will be nicer"?

Bob : Yes, I ___6___ .

Tom : Do you think tomorrow will be nicer?

Bob : No. Tomorrow will ___7___ worse (更糟).

Tom : Why do you think ___8___ ?

Bob : Do you know the "American Confucius"?

Tom : Yes, he is your English teacher. He is old and always looks angry. But I still don't understand.

Bob : Yesterday we had an English test, and I m__9__ a ___10___ of mistakes. And we will have an English class tomorrow morning.

Tom : I see. That's too bad.

6. _____

7. _____

8. _____

9. _____

10. _____

60 時間：20分鐘 ＊ 得分： ／15分

A 請仔細閱讀下面文章，選出最適當的答案，使句意完整。

In recent（最近的）years, success in the implementation（實行）of the government's economic policies（經濟政策）has ___1___ life more enjoyable for us. But ___2___ the same time, our environment（環境）has become heavily ___3___ . ___4___ example, the air in Taipei is now so thick with pollutants（污染物）___5___ officials（官員）have warned people to avoid going outdoors several times.

To solve（解決）this problem, the government and the people must work together and try their best to make our environment pleasant to live in again.

1. (　　) ① become ② made ③ make ④ became
2. (　　) ① in ② for ③ at ④ on
3. (　　) ① pollution ② pollute ③ polluting ④ polluted
4. (　　) ① For ② with ③ In ④ At
5. (　　) ① what ② that ③ which ④ who

B 請仔細閱讀下面文章，將最適當的一個字填入空格中。

Vienna（維也納）is a city _____6_____
music and art. There are many museums,
parks, gardens and palaces（宮殿）there.
Because _____7_____ its beautiful scenery
（風景）, many people like to go there
_____8_____ sightseeing（觀光）. Its coffee
houses are very famous, _____9_____. It
is really a nice city, and a lot of people
enjoy _____10_____ their vacations there.

6. _____

7. _____

8. _____

9. _____

10. _____

In October, there are many holidays.
On Double Tenth my family and I went
to Youth Park. The _____11_____ was fine
in the morning. We saw many beautiful
trees and fl _12_____ in the park. We
also saw many boys _____13_____ frisbee
there. In the afternoon, it became a
little cold. I didn't wear my jacket, so
I _____14_____ a cold. Mother brought
me to see a doctor and I took some
_____15_____.

11. _____

12. _____

13. _____

14. _____

15. _____

61

時間：20分鐘　＊　得分：　　／10分

A 請仔細閱讀下面文章，選出最適當的答案，使句意完整。

On my way to the station（車站）this morning, I saw an old woman ____1____ had a large box on her back and a small ____2____ in her hand. I went up to her and said, "____3____ I help you? These boxes look ____4____ heavy for you." She said, "Yes, please. You are a good boy. Thank you." I took the large box from her back and walked to the station with her.

When we arrived at the station, she said, "____5____ a kind boy you are! Thank you very much." "You're welcome," I said.

I was very happy all the day.

1. (　　) ① who　　② whose　　③ whom　　④ which

2. (　　) ① it　　② one　　③ that　　④ hers

3. (　　) ① Shall　　② Will　　③ Am　　④ Would

4. (　　) ① much　　② more　　③ well　　④ too

5. (　　) ① Who　　② Which　　③ What　　④ How

B 請仔細閱讀下面文章，將最適當的一個字填入空格中。

The lights were red, so the old man stopped his car until they changed ___6___ green. While he was waiting, a police car came up behind him, hit his car hard ___7___ the back and stopped.

There ___8___ two policemen in the police car, and they were very surprised and glad when the old man got ___9___ of his car and walked to them without any trouble. He was about 70 years old.

The old man came to the door of the police car, smiled kindly, and said, "Young man, ___10___ do you stop this car when the lights are red and I am not here?"

6. _____

7. _____

8. _____

9. _____

10. _____

62

時間：20分鐘 ＊ 得分： ／10分

A 請仔細閱讀下面文章，選出最適當的答案，使句意完整。

Lukang（鹿港）citizens were upset _____1_____ Du Pont Company（杜邦公司）making pollution there. An official said 964 persons in Lukang signed a proposal（提議）_____2_____ was about wanting their mayor（市長）"out."

Before the mayor _____3_____ elected（選舉）, he said he wanted to help Lukang's people in their problem with Du Pont Co. But afterwards（以後）, he didn't _____4_____ his promise（諾言）. So Lukang's people were _____5_____ with his behavior（行為）.

1. ( ) ① on ② by ③ in ④ to
2. ( ) ① which ② who ③ whom ④ whose
3. ( ) ① be ② were ③ was ④ is
4. ( ) ① go ② keep ③ make ④ break
5. ( ) ① glad ② joy ③ happy ④ unhappy

B 請仔細閱讀下面文章，將最適當的一個字填入空格中。

Older people may still remember that there was once a time when the Tamsui River（淡水河）was very clean. They may have even s 6 in this river and had a good ____7____ there. But a ____8____ several years, the river has become polluted. Many factories situated（位於）along the Tamsui River pour（倒；灌）polluted waste（廢棄）water into the river. This river has become very d 9 y.

6. _____

7. _____

8. _____

9. _____

10. _____

Our government（政府）is planning to make Taipei's Tamsui River cleaner ____10____ five years. All of the people in Taipei should help our government, and then we will have a clean Tamsui River again.

63

時間：20分鐘　✱　得分：　／15分

A 請仔細閱讀下面文章，選出最適當的答案，使句意完整。

Once upon a time a crow（烏鴉）was very thirsty（渴）. He flew（飛）over the field and woods（森林）. He was looking ____1____ water. But he could not find any. At last he saw a pitcher（水罐）____2____ a little water in ____3____ . He flew down and put his head into the pitcher, but he could not reach the water. He was a

very wise crow and did not give ____4____ . He thought for a while. Then he began picking ____5____ stones and dropping them into the pitcher.

In this way the water rose higher and higher, and at last it came near the top.

1. (　　) ① at ② on ③ for ④ of
2. (　　) ① with ② has ③ in ④ for
3. (　　) ① one ② it ③ there ④ him
4. (　　) ① up ② of ③ at ④ in
5. (　　) ① to ② up ③ with ④ for

B 請仔細閱讀下面文章，將最適當的一個字填入空格中。

My father is a clerk. His office is in this city. He comes home from work ____6____ seven every evening. ____7____ home he likes to sit in his chair and ____8____ television. He is fifty years old. My mother is forty-five. She's very kind and likes to do things for us.

I am thirteen years old. I have ____9____ brother and two sisters. My brother is a high school student. And he wants a car, but he is still too young. We are all at home this evening, because my uncle is here ____10____ Taipei. We are very happy.

6. _____

7. _____

8. _____

9. _____

10. _____

Bill lived ____11____ a farm ____12____ his parents and his little sister Mary. He had no friends to play ____13____ because Mary was too small. So he s ____14____ most of his time playing alone ____15____ the woods and fields.

11. _____

12. _____

13. _____

14. _____

15. _____

64

時間：20分鐘 ＊ 得分： ／15分

A 請仔細閱讀下面文章，選出最適當的答案，使句意完整。

The Kaohsiung City Government（高雄市政府）held a large dance party _____1_____ February 14. Nearly 100,000 students went to the Chiang Kai-shek Gymnasium（體育館）for dancing. Although there only 40,000 _____2_____, the authorities（當局）could not stop those students _____3_____ tickets from going into the gymnasium. The mayor（市長）_____4_____ about 7 p.m. He said that he planned to hold similar activities（活動）weekly in the future. Though the _____5_____ was very small, most students still enjoyed themselves very much.

1. (　　) ① at　　　② in　　　③ on　　　④ for
2. (　　) ① people　② person　③ cars　　④ tickets
3. (　　) ① with　　② without　③ of　　　④ having
4. (　　) ① arrived at　② reached in　③ arrived　④ reached
5. (　　) ① music　　② party　　③ space　　④ dance

B 請仔細閱讀下面文章，將最適當的一個字填入空格中。

A famous nineteenth-century（世紀）traveler described（描寫）Salzburg（薩爾斯堡） __6__ "one of the three most beautiful regions（地區） __7__ earth." __8__ fact, Salzburg is known as the place __9__ Mozart（莫札特）was born. Besides, the city is filled __10__ music, dance, and songs the whole year round. Its scenery（風景）is also wonderful.

__11__ American student Judy came to Taiwan about six months __12__ . She is studying Chinese now. It is easy for her to read Chinese books. __13__ write Chinese is difficult. She wants to speak Chinese, but many people speak to her __14__ English. So her teacher says __15__ he will give her a chance to speak Chinese.

6. _____

7. _____

8. _____

9. _____

10. _____

11. _____

12. _____

13. _____

14. _____

15. _____

65 時間：20分鐘 ＊ 得分： ／15分

A 請仔細閱讀下面文章，選出最適當的答案，使句意完整。

There are many countries in the world. Visiting other countries ___1___ interesting. Do you want to visit a foreign（外國的）country？ Of course you will say you want ___2___ .

You can visit a foreign country you like very soon. Just go to a bookstore and ___3___ some books about the country. When you read them, you can know ___4___ about the people in the country. You can also go to a lot of beautiful places there.

___5___ is fun. If you read books, you can visit countries you like. Please read many books！

1. ( ) ① are ② is ③ being ④ was
2. ( ) ① doing it ② do it ③ to do so ④ doing so
3. ( ) ① look for ② look in
  ③ look into ④ look after
4. ( ) ① many ② several ③ little ④ much
5. ( ) ① Reads books ② Reading books
  ③ Reading on books ④ To read in books

B 請仔細閱讀下面文章，將最適當的一個字填入空格中。

Today ___6___ my father's birthday. He is forty six years ___7___ but he looks younger. He has a lot ___8___ black hair. He likes playing the guitar. He has big ears. He has a good ear ___9___ music. He also likes walking very much, so we gave him shoes as a birthday p__10__ . He was very happy. His eyes became big and bright.

6. _____
7. _____
8. _____
9. _____
10. _____

Koalas（無尾熊）are very pretty a__11__ . They have big ears, small eyes, and black noses. In the day koalas usually s__12__ . ___13___ night they go around and find food. There are lots of koalas __14__ Australia. The people in Australia l__15__ them.

11. _____
12. _____
13. _____
14. _____
15. _____

66 時間：20分鐘 ✱ 得分： /15分

A 請仔細閱讀下面文章，選出最適當的答案，使句意完整。

Foreign students ___1___ participated（參加）in the Chung Cheng Cup Dragon Boat Race（中正杯龍舟賽）burned paper money yesterday. It is said that if one doesn't want to drown（淹死）when ___2___ a river, one must give some paper money ___3___ water ghosts（鬼）. It is even said that a dragon（龍）flies out of a painting after an important man touches its ___4___. Yesterday, a well-___5___ person was invited to dot（點）the eyes of the dragon boats. Everyone hopes that the race will be successful.

1. ( ) ① which ② who were ③ whom ④ who
2. ( ) ① swimming ② is crossing
   ③ through ④ crossing
3. ( ) ① for ② to ③ with ④ as
4. ( ) ① tail ② nose ③ head ④ eyes
5. ( ) ① know ② famous ③ known ④ knowed

B 請仔細閱讀下面文章，將最適當的一個字填入空格中。

_____6_____ television, reading books, and listening _____7_____ music and the radio are the most common things Taipei people do with their leisure（空閒）time. This was found out _____8_____ a public opinion poll（民意測驗）a couple of days ago. The result（結果）of the poll showed that each Taipei citizen s _9_ 13.4 hours a week in recreational activities（娛樂活動）. _____10_____ also showed that Taipei citizens still need more parks, libraries, and children's playgrounds.

After lunch Fred and Dick w 11 to the park. There were many people there. Some were walking a 12 , and others were playing baseball. Fred and Dick _____13_____ tennis. They came home at six. After dinner Fred watched television. Dick _____14_____ to music in his room. About nine Fred went up to his room and _____15_____ English, history, and Chinese. He went to bed at ten.

6. _____

7. _____

8. _____

9. _____

10. _____

11. _____

12. _____

13. _____

14. _____

15. _____

67 時間：20分鐘 ✻ 得分： /10分

A 請仔細閱讀下面文章，選出最適當的答案，使句意完整。

Mr. Lin : You are forty minutes late, John. It's nine ten.
John : I'm sorry, Mr. Lin.
Mr. Lin : You got up late, ___1___ ?
John : Yes, it was already eight when I got up. I hurried ___2___ the bus stop, but I arrived too late ___3___ my bus. So I came by the next one.
Mr. Lin : Why didn't you get up earlier ?
John : Because I went to bed very late and I slept only three hours.
Mr. Lin : Only three hours ? What were you doing ?
John : I ___4___ a book. It was very interesting and I couldn't stop it.
Mr. Lin : Oh, I see. Reading books is very good. But you must not be late again.
John : ___5___ , Mr. Lin. I'll never be late again.

1. (　) ① do you ② did you ③ didn't you ④ don't you
2. (　) ① to ② for ③ by ④ on
3. (　) ① taking ② to take ③ of taking ④ took
4. (　) ① read ② am reading
　　　 ③ was reading ④ had been read
5. (　) ① Yes, I do ② Yes, I won't
　　　 ③ No, I won't ④ No, I don't

B 請仔細閱讀下面文章，將最適當的一個字填入空格中。

Tom and John were boys. They were both twelve years old, and they were ___6___ the same class in their school. Last Friday afternoon they had a fight in class, and their teacher was very angry. He said to both of them, "Stay here after the lessons this afternoon, and write your names a thousand times."

After the last lesson, all the other boys went home. They had no school on Saturday and Sunday, so Tom and John wanted to go home. But they had ___7___ stay in the classroom ___8___ their teacher. They began ___9___ their names.

Then John began crying. The teacher looked at him and said, "Why ___10___ you crying, John?" "Because his name is Tom May, and mine is John Hollingsworth," John said.

6. _____

7. _____

8. _____

9. _____

10. _____

68

時間：20分鐘 ＊ 得分： ／15分

A 請仔細閱讀下面文章，選出最適當的答案，使句意完整。

　　Fast economic development（經濟發展）has greatly improved our life. There are now few people who are too ___1___ to buy food and clothes. Most people are rich, ___2___ they do not seem very happy. Why？ ___3___ we still need to develop our culture（文化）. After school or work, we should read books, ___4___ music, go to cultural centers, or do something relaxing. If we can do these, we will be happier and our society（社會）will be ___5___ peaceful.

1. (　　) ① rich　　② fat　　③ thin　　④ poor
2. (　　) ① and　　② but　　③ so　　④ because
3. (　　) ① And　　② So　　③ Because　　④ But
4. (　　) ① listen　　② listen to　　③ listen at　　④ hear
5. (　　) ① very　　② much　　③ more　　④ very much

B 請仔細閱讀下面文章，將最適當的一個字填入空格中。

Mrs. Wang was worried that she was very fat. "I am too fat," she said to her friend," but I don't know ___6___ to do." Her friend told her to see Dr. Tzeng. "All you need to do ___7___ eat less and exercise more," said Dr. Tzeng. He began to write on a piece of paper. "Eat lots of fruit and v ___8___, and go swimming every day."

A few weeks later, Mrs. Wang's friend visited her. She was surprised to find that Mrs. Wang was ___9___ than before. And she was more surprised to see that she was eating a big sandwich and ice cream. Mrs. Wang said, "I have already had a lot of the food the ___10___ told me to eat. Now I'm eating my own dinner."

6. _____

7. _____

8. _____

9. _____

10. _____

This is a class of boys. They are ___11___ a small classroom. The teacher is at the b ___12___. He is writing on it ___13___ a piece of chalk （粉筆）. The boys' chairs are in a row （排）behind their ___14___. One of the boys ___15___ holding a ruler （尺）.

11. _____

12. _____

13. _____

14. _____

15. _____

69 時間：20分鐘 ✱ 得分： /15分

A 請仔細閱讀下面文章，選出最適當的答案，使句意完整。

Alice : I'm invited to Mary's birthday party this afternoon. May I go to the party, Mother?

Mother : Yes, of course, if you ___1___ busy.

Alice : It begins at three. I'll go out at two o'clock, because I must find a nice present. How about a stamp album (集郵冊)?

Mother : That's a good idea. ___2___ the way, Alice, you must come back before it gets too dark.

Alice : What time must I ___3___ home? Can I stay ___4___ her house until seven thirty?

Mother : ___5___ . You must leave her house by six.

1. (　) ① were ② are ③ be ④ aren't
2. (　) ① On ② By ③ In ④ Of
3. (　) ① came ② coming ③ be coming ④ come
4. (　) ① with ② of ③ at ④ on
5. (　) ① No ② Yes ③ O.K. ④ All right

B 請仔細閱讀下面文章，將最適當的一個字填入空格中。

Mr. Jones was a man ___6___ always forgot to mail letters. One day he ___7___ asked to mail a letter by his wife. She put a piece of paper ___8___ his back. It said, "Ask him to mail a letter." Mr. Jones met some people on the street, and ___9___ told him about the letter. So the letter did not stay ___10___ his pocket (口袋). That was Mrs. Jones's good idea.

6. _____

7. _____

8. _____

9. _____

10. _____

Our school is ___11___ a hill. School begins ___12___ eight forty-five.

Some students go to school ___13___ bicycle. John sometimes gets up late and r __14__ to school.

Mary can't go to school, because she's very s __15__ .

11. _____

12. _____

13. _____

14. _____

15. _____

70 時間：20分鐘 ＊ 得分：　／10分

A 請仔細閱讀下面文章，選出最適當的答案，使句意完整。

Mother ： Mary, I have something ＿＿1＿＿ you. I want you to help me in the kitchen.

Mary ： Oh, Mother! I am going to play tennis this afternoon. We will have a game ＿＿2＿＿ month.

Mother ： I know. But Uncle Jim's family will visit us this evening, you know. You can play tennis tomorrow. So please help me in the kitchen, Mary.

Mary ： All right, Mother. Let's cook a good dinner for them. Is that all?

Mother ： Oh, ＿＿3＿＿ kind you are! Will you go to the shop ＿＿4＿＿ some fruit?

Mary ： Yes, Mother. Then I will go to the shop first, because ＿＿5＿＿ Saturday they close the shop early in the afternoon.

Mother ： Thank you. You are a good girl.

1. (　　) ① ask ② to ask ③ asking ④ ask of
2. (　　) ① last ② at ③ next ④ one
3. (　　) ① what ② what a ③ how about ④ how
4. (　　) ① to buy ② buying ③ bought ④ and bought
5. (　　) ① at ② on ③ for ④ in

B 請仔細閱讀下面文章，將最適當的一個字填入空格中。

I have good news ___6___ you. Last Saturday I played tennis with the best player in my school and I won. You taught me how ___7___ play tennis when I visited you before. At that time I enjoyed it very much. Since then I have practiced hard ___8___ school.

I also ___9___ a very good time with you when I was a small child. You often came to my house and played with me. Then you always listened to the foolish (愚蠢的) stories I wanted to tell you. When you married and left our city, I missed (想念) you very much.

I am going to finish junior high school next month. I would like to come and see you soon and tell you ___10___ my happy school life. Let's play tennis together then.

You have been sick for a week. I hope you will get well soon.

6. ＿＿＿＿＿

7. ＿＿＿＿＿

8. ＿＿＿＿＿

9. ＿＿＿＿＿

10. ＿＿＿＿＿

71 時間：20分鐘 ＊ 得分： ／10分

A 請仔細閱讀下面文章，選出最適當的答案，使句意完整。

Taiwan has four seasons. It also has many places ___1___ have mountains and rivers. Please think about living in ___2___ places. You will find a lot of things you can enjoy.

___3___ early in the morning in spring and walk in the fields. You will see pretty flowers and hear the songs of happy birds. In summer, it will be ___4___ to catch fish in the river. The blue sky in ___5___ is one of the most beautiful things. When you have much snow in winter, you can ski in the mountains.

It is nice to enjoy the four seasons this way, isn't it?

1. (　　) ① which　② and it　③ where　④ and
2. (　　) ① this　② many　③ so　④ such
3. (　　) ① Rising up　　② Get up
　　　　 ③ Getting up　　④ Catch up
4. (　　) ① fun　② funny　③ funning　④ funned
5. (　　) ① fall　② seasons　③ rivers　④ fields

B 請仔細閱讀下面文章，將最適當的一個字填入空格中。

Yesterday I was ___6___ television. At that time I learned that in some countries a lot of people are very h ___7___ and want food. On the television they could not stand up and walk. They were just sitting in their homes or on the streets and w ___8___ for death. It was the first time ___9___ I learned so many people do not have enough food. It was a great surprise to me.

After I watched the program, I said to myself, "Why don't they have enough food? Is there anything I can do for them?" It is not easy for me to find the answer ___10___ these questions. But I want to study this problem. I will be happy if I can help them.

6. _____

7. _____

8. _____

9. _____

10. _____

72

時間：20分鐘 ＊ 得分： ／10分

A 請仔細閱讀下面文章，選出最適當的答案，使句意完整。

Dear Helen,

Father is going to give me a picnic party out at the Sun Moon Lake ＿＿＿1＿＿ my birthday, August 15. He said that I may have seven friends at the party. I want you and your brother John to be two of them. We will go ＿＿2＿＿ and then play games by the lake. I ＿＿3＿＿ that we will have much fun.

Father will ＿＿＿4＿＿＿ on his truck at eight o'clock. We will ＿＿＿5＿＿＿ again by six o'clock. I hope you will be able to come.

Your friend,
Nancy

1. (　) ① at 　　② for 　　③ on 　　④ in
2. (　) ① to fish 　② fishing 　③ on fishing 　④ fish
3. (　) ① am sure 　　　　　② sure
　　　　③ am being sure 　　④ to sure
4. (　) ① drive out us 　　　② drive us out
　　　　③ drive out of us 　　④ drive us
5. (　) ① be home 　　　　② go to home
　　　　③ at home 　　　　④ home

B 請仔細閱讀下面文章，將最適當的一個字填入空格中。

Jiro did not do his English home-work yesterday evening. But he has just done it. I hear him speaking English to an English girl now. The English girl spoken to by him is a senior high school student ___6___ I introduced to him yesterday. He can speak English well. ___7___ a good speaker of English he is! He has been most interested in English of all subjects. Those subjects are Japanese, mathematics, art, history, etc. It is not so easy ___8___ him ___9___ speak English. Today is his 17th birthday. He was born in 1980. I think that he h___10___ better invite her to his birthday party.

6. _____

7. _____

8. _____

9. _____

10. _____

73 時間：20分鐘 ＊ 得分： ／15分

A 請仔細閱讀下面文章，選出最適當的答案，使句意完整。

One day a worker went to the market to buy some fish for his lunch. He ___1___ a fish and ___2___ to his nose.

"Hey! What's this?" asked the seller of the fish. "Why do you smell (聞) that fish? Don't you think it is fresh?"

"I wasn't ___3___ . I was only talking to him."

"Talking to him? I can't believe it!"

"I asked him if there was any news from his home."

"Well, and what did he say to that?"

"He said he didn't get ___4___ news because he ___5___ away from home for more than three days."

1. (　) ① picked of　　　　② picked up
　　　 ③ was picking up　 ④ picked out
2. (　) ① held it up　　　 ② held up it
　　　 ③ holds it up　　　④ held up of it
3. (　) ① smelled　② smelt　③ smelling　④ to smell
4. (　) ① the latest　② the later　③ the late　④ latest
5. (　) ① have been　　　② have
　　　 ③ had been　　　　④ had being

B 請仔細閱讀下面文章，將最適當的一個字填入空格中。

Television has become a way of life: first the children come home from school and sit down ____6____ front of the TV set; then their elders take over after dinner and w__7__ their favorite programs. If you want to stay ____8____ your set without interruption（中斷）, you may have TV dinners.

Television has brought everything ____9____ our home. We should be able to tell good programs ____10____ bad ones.

One day in June, Miss Brown visited Betty's ____11____. Then she came to Betty's class. She showed the students some interesting p__12__ about her country, and they asked her many questions ____13____ English. After that Miss Brown played the ____14____, and the students ____15____ songs. They had a very good time that day.

6. _____

7. _____

8. _____

9. _____

10. _____

11. _____

12. _____

13. _____

14. _____

15. _____

74

時間：20分鐘 ＊ 得分：　　／15分

A 請仔細閱讀下面文章，選出最適當的答案，使句意完整。

Yesterday was Thursday. Tom got up ____1____ six-thirty. In the early morning, he read English ____2____ thirty minutes. After breakfast, he walked to school ____3____ his brother Joe.

Tom was busy yesterday morning. He studied Chinese first. Then he wrote a letter ____4____ his friend John. And he went to the school library and borrowed three books. In the afternoon, he drew a picture and played baseball (棒球) with his friends. After school, he took a bus home.

In the evening, Tom did his homework and studied his lessons. He went to bed at ten-thirty ____5____ .

1. (　　) ① on　　　② at　　　③ in　　　④ for
2. (　　) ① on　　　② at　　　③ in　　　④ for
3. (　　) ① with　　② to　　　③ by　　　④ in
4. (　　) ① with　　② to　　　③ by　　　④ in
5. (　　) ① yesterday morning　　② last week
　　　　③ last night　　　　　　④ tonight

B 請仔細閱讀下面文章，將最適當的一個字填入空格中。

A : Where ___6___ your pen pal live?

B : He lives in England.

A : How ___7___ have you known
him?

B : I've known him for two years.

A : ___8___ the way, aren't you a
member（會員）of the tennis club?

B : ___9___, I am, but it was rainy
yesterday afternoon, so we couldn't
___10___ tennis.

6. _____

7. _____

8. _____

9. _____

10. _____

John is a student. He is ___11___
school. He is ___12___ my class. We
are good friends. My sister is Sue.
She is ___13___ the kitchen. She is
cooking. My father and mother are in
the ___14___ room. They are reading.
They are b ___15___ good teachers.

11. _____

12. _____

13. _____

14. _____

15. _____

75 時間：20分鐘 ＊ 得分： ／15分

A 請仔細閱讀下面文章，選出最適當的答案，使句意完整。

Helen likes to read books very much. She says
___1___ is bad to watch television all evening. She
thinks people living long ago were happier than people
of today, ___2___ they had enough time for reading.

After Helen and Mike read books in the library, they
visited the park to have lunch. In the park they enjoyed
many flowers, fresh green leaves and sweet songs of many
___3___ . Mike thought they
___4___ keep wonderful
nature. On her way home,
Helen bought her father a
present ___5___ his birthday.
He was very glad to have it.

1. (　) ① that　② this　③ it　④ she
2. (　) ① because　② so　③ though　④ but
3. (　) ① fish　② birds　③ dogs　④ cats
4. (　) ① has to　② have to　③ must　④ had to
5. (　) ① for　② in　③ to　④ of

B 請仔細閱讀下面文章，將最適當的一個字填入空格中。

Some people don't use their time well. Sometimes they are very lazy. They are ___6___ quick and careful workers and often ___7___ many mistakes. They usually must do their work several t___8___ , because there are too many mistakes. Such people often can't succeed ___9___ the future. They may f___10___ because of their laziness.

6. _____

7. _____

8. _____

9. _____

10. _____

My name is John. I walk to school ___11___ seven every m___12___ . The first class is at eight-ten. There are twenty-three boys and eighteen girls ___13___ my class. Mr. Lin teaches us English. He is a good t___14___ . We often go home at once ___15___ school.

11. _____

12. _____

13. _____

14. _____

15. _____

My friend is John.

76 時間：20分鐘 ＊ 得分：　　／15分

A 請仔細閱讀下面文章，選出最適當的答案，使句意完整。

Everyone wanted ＿＿1＿＿ be rich. Many men came from every place to find gold（黃金）. They bought all the ground near the river. They made big holes in it, and tried to find more gold.

Tom was one of those men who came to find gold. He was a good man ＿＿2＿＿ worked hard. He bought ＿＿3＿＿ last piece of ground. ＿＿4＿＿ was a long way from the river. No one else wanted to buy it. But Tom spent all his money for it. He worked hard every day, but he never found one piece of gold. After six months he had no money to buy even bread. He was a poor man, ＿＿5＿＿ only a piece of ground.

1. (　　) ① of　　　② in　　　③ to　　　④ at
2. (　　) ① those　② who　　③ which　④ this
3. (　　) ① a　　　② that　　③ this　　④ the
4. (　　) ① That　② It　　　③ These　④ He
5. (　　) ① with　② who　　③ has　　④ have

B 請仔細閱讀下面文章，將最適當的一個字填入空格中。

Hello, friends! I'm John Lee
___6___ America. I came to Taiwan
___7___ January. In America, I
___8___ English at home and school.

In America, you will find a lot of
people who speak English. ___9___
you speak English, you can talk with
them.

I enjoy learning Chinese now. I
want to talk with friends ___10___
Chinese.

Look ___11___ this
picture. The b ___12___
is Bill. The ___13___
is Mary. Bill is a student.
Mary is a ___14___ , too.

Bill is a short boy.
Mary is not short. She
is ___15___ girl. Bill
and Mary are good
students.

6. _____

7. _____

8. _____

9. _____

10. _____

11. _____

12. _____

13. _____

14. _____

15. _____

77

時間：20分鐘 ＊ 得分： ／15分

A 請仔細閱讀下面文章，選出最適當的答案，使句意完整。

We all like sports, many kinds of sports. We can enjoy sports at school, or in the park. We can ___1___ many games on television. ___2___, schoolboys and schoolgirls like sports, too. They are usually in one of the ___3___ in their schools. They play games very hard, even on Sunday.

If students enjoy sports and study hard, they will be better students. It is not easy ___4___ them to have enough time for both sports and studying. ___5___ sports can make strong people, and studying can make good people. Both things are important for students.

1. (　) ① play　　② watch　　③ look　　④ see
2. (　) ① Of course　② Though　③ But　　④ Or
3. (　) ① games　② plays　　③ rooms　④ clubs
4. (　) ① at　　② for　　③ to　　④ by
5. (　) ① But　　② And　　③ Though　④ Or

B 請仔細閱讀下面文章，將最適當的一個字填入空格中。

Bored people learn things s __6__ ly . If they are not interested __7__ a subject, they usually do not __8__ questions. The subject becomes confusing __9__ they do not try to understand it. Then, a bored person becomes a __10__ person .

6. _____

7. _____

8. _____

9. _____

10. _____

These animals are in a __11__ . The m __12__ are on the left. They are not in a cage (籠子). There is a bear further (較遠) away. In the cage near us there is a t __13__ and a __14__ on the right. There is an __15__ further to the right of the picture.

11. _____

12. _____

13. _____

14. _____

15. _____

78

時間：20分鐘 ＊ 得分： ／10分

A 請仔細閱讀下面文章，選出最適當的答案，使句意完整。

I came home ___1___ school at twelve-thirty. After lunch, Father asked me to take our dog Carter for a walk. Carter walked so fast ___2___ I got a little tired.

When I came back, I got a letter from my brother in America.

He said in ___3___ letter, "Three weeks have passed since I came to America. I have made friends with many American students. The English spoken by them is not always clear, ___4___ it is sometimes difficult for me to understand them."

He also said, "I am studying English very hard now. Joe, don't stop ___5___ to the English programs on the radio."

I thought I had to study English much harder.

1. ( ) ① from ② to ③ of ④ at
2. ( ) ① if ② that ③ as ④ when
3. ( ) ① your ② my ③ her ④ his
4. ( ) ① but ② or ③ so ④ that
5. ( ) ① listen ② listened ③ listens ④ listening

B 請仔細閱讀下面文章，將最適當的一個字填入空格中。

Jim went to his friend's farm to buy a horse. He saw a young horse and ___6___ two hundred dollars for it.

Jim gave the horse a lot of food and was very kind to it. It was able to learn quickly, so he taught it to r___7___.

6. _____

7. _____

8. _____

9. _____

10. _____

After two years, the horse was very lazy. It liked to sleep all day, and it didn't want to work. One morning Jim wanted to go to another town and told the horse to pull the cart. But it didn't want to pull the cart. Jim didn't know what to do. Then his brother came out of the house.

"All right," he said. "I have a good ___8___ !" He got a p___9___ of paper and wrote ___10___ it :
DOES ANYONE WANT TO BUY THIS HORSE ?
GOOD DOG'S FOOD

He showed the paper to the horse. When the horse saw the paper, it began to pull the cart. After that, it was never lazy again.

79

時間：20分鐘 ＊ 得分：　　／10分

A 請仔細閱讀下面文章，選出最適當的答案，使句意完整。

Sunday, June 10   Fine

Today was Mother's birthday. I wanted to make breakfast for her.

Mother was very glad ＿＿＿1＿＿＿ she came down and found breakfast on the table.

Father said ＿＿＿2＿＿＿ breakfast, "Mary is so kind to Mother that I'm glad, too. I'll take Mother and you ＿＿＿3＿＿＿ the art museum（美術館）this afternoon."

We arrived there at two o'clock. There were many pictures painted by famous artists. Mother liked some of ＿＿＿4＿＿＿ very much, and Father bought a copy （複製品） of the picture she liked ＿＿＿5＿＿＿.

1. (　) ① when　② that　③ which　④ where
2. (　) ① on　② in　③ at　④ to
3. (　) ① to　② in　③ off　④ out
4. (　) ① they　② it　③ picture　④ them
5. (　) ① well　② good　③ better　④ best

B 請仔細閱讀下面文章，將最適當的一個字填入空格中。

The Taipei Zoo at Mucha (木柵) was bursting (爆滿) ___6___ New Year's Day with one hundred thousand visitor or ___7___. It is said ___8___ children under six who did not have to buy tickets numbered another twenty thousand.

I took my children to the new zoo ___9___ public bus the next day. We saw elephants, lions, tigers, monkeys, rabbits and all kinds of birds.

The children did as the signs everywhere said : Be kind to animals. Don't feed them. Put the trash in the trash can, not ___10___ the ground.

We all had a lot of fun.

6. _____

7. _____

8. _____

9. _____

10. _____

80 時間：20分鐘 ＊ 得分： ／15分

A 請仔細閱讀下面文章，選出最適當的答案，使句意完整。

Have you ever visited an airport? It is often a very interesting place. An airport is usually ＿＿1＿＿ of people. Some of them will be passengers（乘客）. Some have just arrived by plane and they are now waiting for a car or a bus or a train to take them home. ＿＿2＿＿ are waiting to go on planes ＿＿3＿＿ will take them to another city or another country. They are buying books ＿＿4＿＿ read on the plane or talking to their friends or relatives（親戚）. Many of the people at the airport are not passengers. They have come to meet passengers who are going to arrive or to say good-bye to friends or relatives who are going to ＿＿5＿＿.

1. (　　) ① made　　② built　　③ by way　　④ full
2. (　　) ① They　　② Another　　③ The other　　④ Others
3. (　　) ① which　　② but　　③ and that　　④ and
4. (　　) ① on　　② in　　③ for　　④ to
5. (　　) ① jump　　② tell　　③ leave　　④ show

B 請仔細閱讀下面文章，將最適當的一個字填入空格中。

Nancy : What day ___6___ you think it is today, George?

George : It's Friday, isn't it?

Nancy : Yes, it is, and today is my birthday, too. I've got a card ___7___ my mother, but n___8___ from you.

George : I'm sorry that I forgot your birthday, dear. ___9___ is difficult to remember it because ⋯ you n___10___ look older.

6. _____

7. _____

8. _____

9. _____

10. _____

I have a pen friend ___11___ name is Helen. She lives in Tainan.

She came to see me last Sunday. It was a very nice day. We went to Tamsui. We were able to see some islands far away. We saw small ships which were sailing ___12___ the sea. A ___13___ the seaside there ___14___ many trees, and they were also beautiful.

I was very happy to take her to s___15___ a wonderful place.

11. _____

12. _____

13. _____

14. _____

15. _____

⏰ 克漏字答題技巧 ——

1. 趕快把文章瀏覽一遍，掌握全文大意，並將關鍵字圈出。

2. 把選項依序套入空格中，根據句意選出最適合的答案，注意時式、單複數及單字詞類的變化。

3. 不會的題目，先刪掉確定錯誤的項目，再憑「語感」去猜，不要放著不做。

✳ 每回測驗的練習時間為20分鐘，測驗題目分為10和15題兩種；錯誤的題數在五分之一以內即為優等，三分之一以內須再接再厲，二分之一以上須將題目重覆練習。每作完一個 Test，務必參考詳解，找出錯誤所在，力求完全理解。

PART · II
歷屆聯考試題

八十五年度台北市公立高中聯招試題

A 請仔細閱讀下面文章，選出最適當的答案，使句意完整。

It's six o'clock now. My mother _____1_____ in the kitchen. She is not only a good mother _____2_____ a modern woman. Many of her skirts are even shorter than _____3_____ . She enjoys _____4_____ with her friends on the weekends. Buying new and beautiful clothes always _____5_____ them. However, after shopping for a whole evening last Sunday, Mother came back home without anything, and _____6_____ did her friend, Jill. I asked them _____7_____ anything was wrong. They said that they were _____8_____ tired that they left the bags on the bus. My mom also told me _____9_____ any word about it to Dad, who would laugh at her. I love my mom. She's a lovely woman, _____10_____ ?

1. ( ) ① cook ② cooks
   ③ cooked ④ is cooking
2. ( ) ① and ② or ③ but ④ as
3. ( ) ① I ② me ③ my ④ mine
4. ( ) ① shop ② shops ③ shopped ④ shopping
5. ( ) ① excite ② excites ③ excited ④ exciting
6. ( ) ① either ② neither ③ too ④ also
7. ( ) ① if ② that ③ where ④ what

8. (　) ① very　② as　③ so　④ such

9. (　) ① don't say　② not to say
　　③ didn't say　④ not saying

10. (　) ① isn't she　② doesn't she
　　③ don't I　④ am I not

My mother was very sad when Dad ____11____ her 40th birthday. She felt that Dad ____12____ , and she was not happy. When we told Dad of this, he laughed and said to Mom, "Maria, how can I remember your birthday when you never seem to look any ____13____ ?" Dad's answer made Mom very ____14____ . Yes, just as Mom said later, "How could one still be angry after that ?"

11. (　) ① decided　② changed
　　③ remembered　④ forgot

12. (　) ① loved her more and more
　　② wanted to give her a surprise
　　③ didn't care about her anymore
　　④ was the best husband in the world

13. (　) ① older　② stronger　③ better　④ taller

14. (　) ① sad　② happy　③ angry　④ bored

Sue's last week's party was the best one she has ever had. All the children who went to the party thought so, too. It was very interesting because her mother had planned ____15____ different for her.

Sue's mother baked ten cakes for each of Sue's friends. She also gave them cream, cookies, fruit, and sugar（糖）powder to put ____16____ their cakes. The children used all these things to make their cakes as ____17____ as they could. The one who made the best-looking cake would be given a special present.

The children had a ____18____ time. They had fun trying to make their own cakes different from others'. They had the best time, ____19____, when they ate the delicious cakes.

15. (　　) ① nothing　　　　② something
　　　　　③ anything　　　　④ few things
16. (　　) ① through　② off　　③ on　　④ under
17. (　　) ① fast　　② similar　③ cheap　④ beautiful
18. (　　) ① bad　　② hard　　③ good　　④ short
19. (　　) ① of course　　　　② for example
　　　　　③ first　　　　　　④ sometimes

How much time do you spend watching TV every day? Would you watch more if there ___20___ more channels (頻道)? About five years ago, most families in Taiwan had only three channels to choose from. Television came into homes through an aerial (天線) which was on the roof (頂部) of the ___21___. Things have changed, however. Cable TV (有線電視) comes into people's homes through cables and gives us a lot more ___22___ than before. Some Cable TV companies have over 60 channels and work 24 hours a ___23___. We need to pay some money to put cables into our homes and the cost sometimes is very high. ___24___, people don't seem to care too much about the money they have to pay ___25___ the cable TV, and this is why I believe we'll see more and more of it in the future.

20. (　) ① is ② have ③ had ④ were
21. (　) ① schools ② offices ③ stores ④ houses
22. (　) ① fables ② programs
　　　　③ activities ④ magazines
23. (　) ① day ② week ③ month ④ year
24. (　) ① So ② However
　　　　③ Finally ④ Especially
25. (　) ① to ② by ③ for ④ with

八十五年度台灣省暨高雄市公立高中聯招試題

A 請仔細閱讀下面文章，選出最適當的答案，使句意完整。

Dear John :

I haven't written to you for a long time. ___1___ everything? I'm going to graduate in June, ___2___ I'm not very happy. Do you know why? I'm going to have a very important exam on the 8th and the 9th of July. If I don't ___3___ in the exam, I won't be able to go to senior high school. So I have to study very hard. My parents want me to exercise. I know that being ___4___ is very important, but I'm really worried about the exam. Sometimes I am quite ___5___. Would you please tell me what I should do?

Your friend,
Jack

1. (　　) ① What's ② How's ③ Where's ④ Who's
2. (　　) ① but ② and ③ since ④ if
3. (　　) ① waste my time ② get into trouble
　　　　③ change my mind ④ get good grades
4. (　　) ① honest ② simple ③ healthy ④ special
5. (　　) ① confused ② interested
　　　　③ broken ④ understood

Did you ever ride a motorcycle? We often feel it's not ___6___ to find a parking space for a car in a big city, but we can easily find ___7___ if we ride a motorcycle. Besides, motorcycles don't ___8___ as much money as cars. However, many young people enjoy riding them very fast. It may be exciting, but it's ___9___. Some people get hurt or even die because they ride motorcycles too fast. We believe that they are really conveniences in our life ___10___ we ride them carefully.

6. (　　) ① easy　　② hard　　③ right　　④ wrong
7. (　　) ① this　　② it　　③ one　　④ that
8. (　　) ① spend　　② cost　　③ take　　④ save
9. (　　) ① noisy　　　　　② convenient
　　　　 ③ comfortable　　④ dangerous
10. (　　) ① although　② before　③ even if　④ as long as

八十五年度北區五年制專科學校聯招試題

A 請仔細閱讀下面文章，選出最適當的答案，使句意完整。

_____1_____ winter and summer vacations, many special activities _____2_____ camping, mountain climbing, and grass skiing, _____3_____ for young people. Some people go camping to learn to live without modern conveniences like electricity. By joining these _____4_____, people not only learn about nature but also learn to _____5_____ things with other people.

1. (　) ① During　② Until　③ When　④ For
2. (　) ① such that　② as so　③ such as　④ alike
3. (　) ① holding
　　　　③ are held
　　　　② held
　　　　④ which hold
4. (　) ① tickets
　　　　③ inventions
　　　　② mistakes
　　　　④ programs
5. (　) ① bother　② think　③ share　④ please

No one can learn a language well _____6_____ a good dictionary. It is an important tool and it will tell you not only _____7_____ a word means but how it is used. As a language changes with time, a good dictionary needs

____8____ about ____9____ . A good dictionary will tell you many interesting facts, like the pronunciation and meanings of a word. It will also tell you how a simple word can be used in different ways. So before you use a dictionary, ____10____ sure to read the front part to learn how to use it well.

6. (　　) ① with ② for ③ without ④ by
7. (　　) ① what ② how ③ who ④ which
8. (　　) ① change ② changed
③ to change ④ to be changed
9. (　　) ① each ten year ② for ten years
③ every ten years ④ other ten years
10. (　　) ① to be ② being ③ it is ④ be

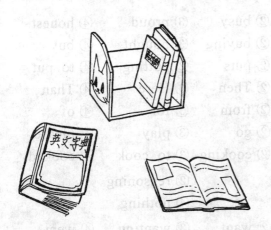

八十五年度中區五年制專科學校聯招試題

A 請仔細閱讀下面文章，選出最適當的答案，使句意完整。

It was two weeks before Christmas, and Mrs. Smith was very _____1_____. She _____2_____ a lot of Christmas cards to send to her friends and to her husband's friends, and _____3_____ them on the table in the living room. _____4_____, when her husband came home from work, she said to him, "Here are the Christmas cards _____5_____ our friends, and here is a pen. Will you _____6_____ write the cards and send them to the post office because I am busy _____7_____ the dinner?" Mr. Smith did not say _____8_____, but walked out of the living room and _____9_____ out of the house. Mrs. Smith was very angry with him, but she did not say anything, _____10_____.

1. (　) ① strong ② busy ③ proud ④ honest
2. (　) ① buys ② buying ③ bought ④ buy
3. (　) ① put ② puts ③ putting ④ to put
4. (　) ① There ② Then ③ Here ④ Than
5. (　) ① with ② from ③ for ④ of
6. (　) ① come ② go ③ play ④ please
7. (　) ① cook ② cooking ③ to cook ④ cooked
8. (　) ① anything ② reasoning
   ③ something ④ nothing
9. (　) ① won't ② want ③ wanting ④ went
10. (　) ① neither ② nor ③ either ④ too

八十五年度南區五年制專科學校聯招試題

A 請仔細閱讀下面文章，選出最適當的答案，使句意完整。

Andy Lau is more popular than ____1____ Chinese singer. Neither Jackie Chan nor Wang Fei has sold more CDs than him. Everyone knows ____2____ . Anyone who listens to him ____3____ will fall in love with him, and any song ____4____ by him will ____5____ popular.

1. (　　) ① any other　　　② the other
　　　　 ③ other　　　　　④ another
2. (　　) ① who is he　　　② whom is he
　　　　 ③ who he is　　　　④ whom he is
3. (　　) ① to sing　② singing　③ sang　　　④ song
4. (　　) ① sings　　② sang　　③ which sings　④ sung
5. (　　) ① let　　　② feel　　③ become　　④ bring

A : I want to ____6____ , but I don't know how to do it.
B : Just think about all the air pollution you make.
A : That's no good. I still can't stop ____7____ about smoking.
B : Then think about all the money you ____8____ on your bad habit.
A : You're not much help.
B : Well, if I ____9____ a doctor, maybe I ____10____ you.

6. (　　) ① give up to smoke　② give smoking up
　　　　③ give up smoking　④ giving up smoking

7. (　　) ① thinking　　　　② to think
　　　　③ to thinking　　　④ think

8. (　　) ① cost　② take　③ spend　④ make

9. (　　) ① am　② have been　③ am to be　④ were

10. (　　) ① can help　　　　② could help
　　　　③ could had helped　④ can have helped

八十四年度台北市公立高中聯招試題

A 請仔細閱讀下面文章，選出最適當的答案，使句意完整。

　　Many people like to collect things. Some collect cups, some collect books, and some collect baseball cards. A long time ago, the Grimm brothers decided to collect ___1___ . They walked from farm to farm with their backpacks. They asked around to find old people who would ___2___ and tell the old stories. Every time a story was told, they tried to write it down with the ___3___ words that the old men used.

　　After five years of hard work, the Grimms collected 86 stories. Their ___4___ book of old stories came out that year. Then they wrote two more books. All through their life, the Grimms collected 210 stories. Today, children all over the world are enjoying these stories ___5___ children 150 years ago.

　　Have you ever read *The Frog Prince*? It's also from the Grimm's books.

1. (　　) ① backpacks ② facts ③ songs ④ stories
2. (　　) ① learn ② record ③ remember ④ understand
3. (　　) ① cute ② good ③ last ④ same
4. (　　) ① best ② first ③ latest ④ only
5. (　　) ① as early as ② as long as
　　　　　③ as much as ④ as soon as

Choosing a present is never easy for me. Last week, _____6_____, it didn't take me a long time to buy my son a birthday present. I bought him a computer game. At the _____7_____, when I took out the machine, everyone was so excited that they wanted to try it right away. I turned it on and waited and waited, but _____8_____ happened, so I decided to try to fix it. While I was doing it, I heard many different ideas, _____9_____ "Push that button!" "Maybe the TV is broken!" and "Why don't you try that first?" Suddenly I found out the problem. I forgot to plug it in! I did it very quickly when nobody was _____10_____. As my son started to play the computer game, I heard someone say to him, "Your father is great! He fixed the machine so quickly!"

6. (　) ① besides ② however
　　　 ③ for example ④ of course

7. (　) ① factory ② party ③ school ④ store

8. (　) ① anything ② everything
　　　 ③ nothing ④ something

9. (　) ① especially ② even ③ like ④ without

10. (　) ① fixing ② looking ③ playing ④ trying

It is very important to know how to recycle trash. First, we can put different kinds of trash into different trash cans. ___11___ , workers in trash trucks pick them up and take them to some special places. There, paper, Coke cans, glass bottles, and plastic things are ___12___ away to different factories.

In these factories, Coke cans and glass bottles are recycled to become new ones. The ___13___ paper is changed into new paper. And plastic things are made into ___14___ and picnic tables. Now, recycling is becoming more ___15___ because we believe it can help us make our world a better place to live.

11. (　　) ① Often　　　　　　② Sometimes
　　　　　③ Then　　　　　　 ④ For example
12. (　　) ① given　② kept　③ sent　④ washed
13. (　　) ① broken　② burned　③ dried　④ used
14. (　　) ① benches　　　　　② magazines
　　　　　③ matches　　　　　④ towels
15. (　　) ① convenient　　　　② expensive
　　　　　③ original　　　　　④ popular

八十四年度台灣省暨高雄市公立高中聯招試題

A 請仔細閱讀下面文章，選出最適當的答案，使句意完整。

A lot of boys in Sue's class love basketball. When an important game is played ___1___ they are in school, some of them will take their Walkmans to school. Between classes, they will ___2___ the radio and talk loudly about the game. One day, Sue complained about the boys' ___3___ but they just laughed and said she ___4___ basketball. "If that is true," Sue said to them, "then you don't understand ___5___ either, because you also complain when girls talk loudly about popular songs."

1. (　) ① while　② where　③ before　④ after
2. (　) ① look at　② look up　③ turn on　④ turn off
3. (　) ① grades　② answers　③ noise　④ knowledge
4. (　) ① understands　　② understood
　　　　③ won't understand　④ didn't understand
5. (　) ① movie　② music　③ menu　④ message

B 請仔細閱讀下面文章，將最適當的一個字填入空格中。

(1) will　　　　　(2) by bus　　　(3) old enough
(4) cares about　(5) could　　　(6) by train
(7) too young　　(8) worried about

Ken is a junior high school student. He usually goes to school ___6___. He does not like it because he often has to wait for a long time. When one of his classmates gets a motorcycle, Ken dreams about one, too. "If I had a motorcycle, I ___7___ save a lot of time." But he knows he is not ___8___ to ride a motorcycle. He also knows if he rides one, his parents will be ___9___ him, especially when traffic is so busy here. So Ken will still take the bus because he ___10___ his parents' feelings.

C 讀完整篇後，請填入適當的字。

Sara Lin and her parents like to go to the department store on weekends. ___11___ of them have something to do there. Mr. Lin can read in the bookstore. Mrs. Lin can go shopping, and Sara can go to a movie. Then they will get t___12___ again at a restaurant to have dinner. H___13___ , they are troubled by one thing--it is usually hard to ___14___ their car near the department store. They can have fun only after they have ___15___ some time trying to find a parking space.

11. _____

12. _____

13. _____

14. _____

15. _____

八十四年度北區五年制專科學校聯招試題

A 請仔細閱讀下面文章，選出最適當的答案，使句意完整。

Everyone needs to eat ____1____ if he or she wants to have a strong body. Our ____2____ also need a kind of food. This kind of food is knowledge. There are ____3____ of getting knowledge. We can learn by reading and thinking about things. If we get knowledge ____4____ our own, we can learn more and ____5____ .

1. (　) ① good ② too ③ well ④ many
2. (　) ① irons ② natures ③ minds ④ interests
3. (　) ① much kind ② many kinds
　　　 ③ much way ④ many ways
4. (　) ① on ② by ③ in ④ for
5. (　) ① best ② better ③ good ④ well

____6____ the summer vacation, there are often many interesting and exciting activities ____7____ young people ____8____ . For example, hiking, camping, swimming, and mountain climbing. Besides being fun, ____9____ is a good way to learn with people ____10____ you have never met before. That's why many students like these activities so much.

6. (　　) ① With　　② On　　③ During　　④ When

7. (　　) ① with　　② in　　③ to　　④ for

8. (　　) ① joining　　② to join
　　　　　③ who take part　　④ who enjoy

9. (　　) ① which　　② it　　③ what　　④ so

10. (　　) ① where　　② which　　③ what　　④ whom

八十四年度中區五年制專科學校聯招試題

A 請仔細閱讀下面文章，選出最適當的答案，使句意完整。

This Pizza House may have seven or eight kinds of pizzas on their ___1___. Would you ___2___ one or two of them?

1. (　) ① picnic　　　　② menu
　　　　③ soccer　　　　④ apartment
2. (　) ① order　② satisfy　③ breathe　④ forget

Many countries are making new ___3___ in order to fight pollution. New products we use in our homes, like color ___4___, washing machines, and cooking tools, must not only produce less pollution but also work better and save more ___5___.

3. (　) ① glasses　② laughs　③ bridges　④ laws
4. (　) ① elephants　　　② noodles
　　　　③ televisions　　④ dictionaries
5. (　) ① flashlight　　　② calendar
　　　　③ electricity　　④ electronics

This spring we really had a good time ___6___ my family stayed in the country. We had taken a house on a river. The water ran right below our windows and flew over big rocks and stones（石頭）that made a kind of ___7___ and made us able ___8___ anytime we liked. I think it was the river ___9___ satisfied all our need during the vacation. It also spoke the reason ___10___ we decided to take the house. It was a good ___11___ from the city life to look at those happy wild animals and other natural lives through the windows clearly ___12___ our own eyes and ___13___ the easy flow of the waters comfortably with our own ears. Although Father and Mother, like other ___14___, asked us not to swim in and near the river because it might be very dangerous, we still had great fun while watching some good-looking birds ___15___ "wild strangers", red and yellow in color, flying and swimming over the pond and river in back of our house. We really like to share the fine feeling with our friends. So we plan to visit the same place for the coming summer. How about joining the plan to enjoy a happy summer time with us？

6. (　　) ① but　　② always　　③ when　　④ besides
7. (　　) ① pond　　② baseball　　③ bedroom　　④ bakery
8. (　　) ① to fish　② to fishing　③ fishing　　④ fished

```
 9. (    ) ① this        ② what        ③ that        ④ where
10. (    ) ① who         ② what        ③ which       ④ why
11. (    ) ① choose      ② change      ③ catch       ④ powder
12. (    ) ① at          ② on          ③ without     ④ with
13. (    ) ① listening to              ② listen to
           ③ listened to               ④ listens to
14. (    ) ① plants                    ② animals
           ③ parents                   ④ cockroaches
15. (    ) ① called      ② calls       ③ calling     ④ call
```

八十四年度南區五年制專科學校聯招試題

A 請仔細閱讀下面文章，選出最適當的答案，使句意完整。

Many people today do not like to waste a lot of time eating. They would often ___1___ fast food. They would usually ___2___ and would often drive to a fast-food restaurant. They would not waste time ___3___ a parking space, but would let their car ___4___ in front of the restaurant ___5___ they are inside.

1. (　) ① feel like to eat　　② feel like eat
　　　　③ feel like eating　　④ like to eating

2. (　) ① go slow　　　　　② be in a hurry
　　　　③ be in no hurry　　④ to take their time

3. (　) ① looking for　　　② looking at
　　　　③ looking after　　④ looking up

4. (　) ① to sit　② sat　　③ sitting　④ sit

5. (　) ① what　② how　③ while　④ that

八十三年度台北市公立高中聯招試題

A 請仔細閱讀下面文章，選出最適當的答案，使句意完整。

Soccer is an interesting sport. It is different from other ___1___ because most players may not use their hands when playing. Playing soccer can develop a strong mind and healthy ___2___. It is also a ___3___ sport in which players must help each other. Do you know that the 1994 World Cup is held in the U.S. right now? So many people around the world are ___4___ about the games and they all hope the team of their own country would win. ___5___ you watch the exciting games on TV, do you hope that some day we can also see the Chinese team play in the World Cup?

1. (　　) ① people　② places　③ players　④ sports
2. (　　) ① body　② hand　③ head　④ man
3. (　　) ① fast　② free　③ team　④ tiring
4. (　　) ① bored　② confused　③ excited　④ surprised
5. (　　) ① Because　② But　③ Until　④ When

We have finally made our apartment look like a new one! Mother has painted the walls light blue, ___6___ our place feels cooler in summer. Father has fixed all our windows and can keep them open ___7___ letting bugs fly inside. Our little garden is ___8___ with beautiful flowers and green plants. It sounds quite ___9___ , doesn't it? I'm sure you will ___10___ our apartment, too. Why don't you come to see it yourself when you have time?

6. (   ) ① because   ② but   ③ or   ④ so
7. (   ) ① by   ② from   ③ in   ④ without
8. (   ) ① filled   ② full   ③ made   ④ satisfied
9. (   ) ① modern   ② nice   ③ noisy   ④ terrible
10. (   ) ① find   ② fix   ③ like   ④ paint

There are living languages and also dead languages. A language people don't speak ___11___ is called a dead language. Latin is ___12___ a language. A living language will grow and change with time. Fifty years ago, people said the word "often" without pronouncing the letter "t." But now many people would ___13___ the pronunciation of that letter. Originally, "wife" meant just a ___14___ . But today a man can't call any woman on the street "wife." So we can say ___15___ is a living language. Can you see the Chinese we use now is also different from that used a hundred years ago?

11. (   ) ① anymore   ② loudly   ③ much   ④ often
12. (   ) ① just   ② not   ③ only   ④ such
13. (   ) ① forget   ② keep   ③ make   ④ miss
14. (   ) ① child   ② husband   ③ man   ④ woman
15. (   ) ① Cantonese ② Chinese   ③ English ④ Latin

Mr. Brown was the owner of a big bookstore. Every day many of his _____16_____ passed his front door and some of them stopped to ask him, "What _____17_____ is it, please?" After several months, Mr. Brown said to himself, "I will stop _____18_____ all those people. I am going to buy a big _____19_____ and put it up in front of my store." But _____20_____ that, a lot of people still stopped every day, looked at the clock, and asked "Is that clock right?"

16. ( ) ① children ② clerks ③ neighbors ④ students
17. ( ) ① day ② month ③ time ④ year
18. ( ) ① answering ② answered
　　　　 ③ and answer ④ to answer
19. ( ) ① calendar ② clock ③ diary ④ dog
20. ( ) ① after ② before ③ between ④ until

You may like to know this new and surprising idea from some doctors. They now say that eating _____21_____ is good for you. Many doctors have studied our _____22_____ habits and got the exciting idea. Most people eat three big meals（餐）a day, but people will be much healthier if they have five or six _____23_____ meals a day. They say our bodies can be better if we eat _____24_____ food every meal. It is even all right to eat ice cream or cookies sometimes. You must not have _____25_____ snacks at one time. Of course, you should always have enough important foods too, like fruits and vegetables.

21. (　　) ① fruits　　② meat　　③ snacks　　④ vegetables
22. (　　) ① dressing　② eating　　③ sleeping　④ study
23. (　　) ① big　　　② good　　③ happy　　④ small
24. (　　) ① less　　　② natural　③ no　　　④ more
25. (　　) ① a lot of　　　　　　② a part of
　　　　　③ some of　　　　　　④ too few

八十三年度台灣省暨高雄市公立高中聯招試題

A 請仔細閱讀下面文章，選出最適當的答案，使句意完整。

Mr. Li is a person who complains a lot. He is never ____1____ with anything. Yesterday he had dinner with his wife in a ____2____. He thought that it was too noisy there and ____3____ to go home. After they went home, his wife started cooking. When they had dinner, Mr. Li got ____4____ again. He didn't think that the food was delicious. His wife stopped eating and ____5____ all the food. Mr. Li had nothing to eat. Finally he understood that he shouldn't complain so much.

1. (　) ① satisfy　　　　　　　② to satisfy
　　　③ satisfying　　　　　④ satisfied
2. (　) ① restaurant　② hospital　③ bakery　④ kitchen
3. (　) ① forgot　② decided　③ knew　④ worried
4. (　) ① happy　② kind　③ angry　④ hurt
5. (　) ① turned off　　　　　② took off
　　　③ kept away　　　　　④ threw away

B 請仔細閱讀下面文章，將最適當的一個字填入空格中。

(1) do　　　　　(2) favorite　　　(3) dangerous
(4) everywhere　(5) for example　(6) in a hurry
(7) count in my head　　　　(8) tell the truth

Many people choose to live in the city because it is more convenient. But if you want me to ___6___, I would say I don't like city life. There are some reasons for this. First, city people are always ___7___. They do not have enough time to care about others. Second, the traffic is so terrible that it is ___8___ to walk or ride a bike on the busy streets. Third, I am worried about the pollution problems in the city. The air is dirty, the water is polluted and there are plastic bags ___9___. Finally, I hate the noise in the city. I need a quieter place to ___10___ most of my studying. I really hope to live in the country.

C 讀完整篇後，請填入適當的字。

The summer vacation is coming and John is excited. He can always use his free time well. He enjoys learning new things ___11___ they are easy or not. This summer, he wants to go camping and learn how to live ___12___ any modern conveniences. He would also like to visit his pen pal, Ken, ___13___ he has never met before. B___14___, he wants to read a lot of books to get more k___15___. Most important of all, he will join some good activities to develop a strong body and mind. He is sure that his summer vacation will be full of fun.

11. _____

12. _____

13. _____

14. _____

15. _____

八十三年度北區五年制專科學校聯招試題

A 請仔細閱讀下面文章，選出最適當的答案，使句意完整。

One day John and Tom went to a restaurant for dinner. The restaurant was very quiet, but they were talking and ___1___ . A woman ___2___ in back of them looked ___3___ at them and said coldly, "___4___ you mind ___5___ so noisy, please?"

1. (　) ① laugh ② laughing ③ to laugh ④ laughed
2. (　) ① who sit ② sat ③ was sitting ④ sitting
3. (　) ① happily ② happy ③ angrily ④ angry
4. (　) ① Would ② Should ③ Most ④ Did
5. (　) ① being not ② not to be
　　　　③ to be ④ not being

Many people visit the park every day. There ___6___ many tall trees and beautiful flowers. They often talk and laugh ___7___ they are in the park. If they eat lunch there, they always pick ___8___ the trash and put ___9___ in the trash can. They always ___10___ .

6. (　) ① have ② is ③ are ④ seem
7. (　) ① and ② during ③ but ④ while
8. (　) ① above ② for ③ up ④ to
9. (　) ① it ② its ③ them ④ his
10. (　) ① on their own ② put it on
　　　　③ keep the park clean ④ having a good time

八十三年度中區五年制專科學校聯招試題

A 請仔細閱讀下面文章，選出最適當的答案，使句意完整。

Some students use their time well. They are quick young men. They don't think about many things at a time. They usually do their ___1___ quickly and nicely. Then they can play ___2___ of the house.

1. (　) ① visits ② questions ③ homework ④ heart
2. (　) ① outside ② happily ③ deliciously ④ together

When Betty was eleven years old, her mother gave her a birthday ___3___ and wanted Betty to ask three friends to come to the house. The mother's ___4___ is to have two ___5___ , four sweet cakes and some coke for each child to eat and drink.

3. (　) ① presents ② party ③ pencil ④ product
4. (　) ① plan ② piano ③ plant ④ plants
5. (　) ① radios ② fruit ③ orders ④ sandwiches

Welcome to have a picnic in the park! But after the picnic, please remember to place your trash ___6___ the large cans in the park or bring them home because we should keep our park as ___7___ as ___8___ houses.

6. (　) ① in　　② near　　③ besides　　④ there
7. (　) ① clean　② clear　　③ cleaned　　④ cleanly
8. (　) ① ourselves'　　　　② ourselve's
　　　　③ our own　　　　　④ our won

Many people who like watching or reading about sports also enjoy _____9_____ them. They like playing sports _____10_____ they have free time, even after a _____11_____ day at school or work.

9. (　) ① playing　② play　　③ plays　　④ to play
10. (　) ① where　② that　　③ who　　④ when
11. (　) ① tired　② tiring　　③ tire　　④ tiringly

We should go to work _____12_____ bus or with our friends in the same car. There will be less pollution and better traffic if there are _____13_____ people _____14_____ on the streets. It's never _____15_____ late to fight pollution.

12. (　) ① in　　② by　　③ on　　④ with
13. (　) ① fewer　② less　　③ least　　④ a few
14. (　) ① drive　② drivers　③ drove　　④ driving
15. (　) ① to　　② as　　③ too　　④ be

八十三年度南區五年制專科學校聯招試題

A 請仔細閱讀下面文章，選出最適當的答案，使句意完整。

　　Aesop's fables are animal stories ＿＿1＿＿ teach important lessons to people. No one knows for sure where these stories came from, but many believe that a man ＿＿2＿＿ Aesop lived about 2,500 years ＿＿3＿＿. And he told people the stories. Why do people enjoy Aesop's fables so much? Maybe they teach us ＿＿4＿＿ ＿＿5＿＿ to find the answers to hard problems.

1. (　　) ① who　　　② which　　　③ whose　　　④ where

2. (　　) ① calls　　　　　　　② was called
　　　　 ③ called　　　　　　　④ who called

3. (　　) ① before　② past　　③ last year　④ ago

4. (　　) ① to think　　　　　② thinking
　　　　 ③ to be thought　　　④ to say

5. (　　) ① care　　　　　　　② careful
　　　　 ③ carefully　　　　　④ be careful

八十二年度台北市公立高中聯招試題

A 請仔細閱讀下面文章，選出最適當的答案，使句意完整。

All students need to have good study habits. When you have good study habits, you learn things ___1___. You also remember them easily.

Do you like to study in the ___2___? This is not a good place because it is usually too noisy. You need to study in a quiet place, like your bedroom. A quiet place will help you only think about one ___3___, and you will learn better.

Before you begin to study, do not forget to clean your ___4___. A good desk light is ___5___, too. You will feel tired easily if there is not enough light.

1. (　) ① coldly　② generally　③ quickly　④ slowly
2. (　) ① bedroom　　　② car
　　　③ library　　　　④ living room
3. (　) ① person　② place　③ teacher　④ thing
4. (　) ① bed　② desk　③ garden　④ house
5. (　) ① expensive　② heavy　③ important　④ special

The most exciting sports are team sports. They are often played and watched by thousands of people. Most people are interested in ___6___ their favorite team. They love to see them win. But even if they ___7___, they will still be liked.

Tickets to important games are not easily ___8___.
Important games are often watched by many people at
home on holidays. When important games are played
during the ___9___, they are often listened to at work
on the radio. People who do this often do not finish
their ___10___, and they don't care. They only care
about their favorite team.

6. (　) ① buying　② hearing　③ playing　④ watching
7. (　) ① leave　　② lose　　③ play　　④ win
8. (　) ① bought　② found　③ sold　　④ won
9. (　) ① day　　② week　　③ month　④ year
10. (　) ① class　　② game　　③ program　④ work

It's not easy to stop smoking. Many people who stop
smoking will smoke again. At a party or at work, they
often find it hard to control themselves and ___11___
to smoke "just one" cigarette. Then, another cigarette,
and another. ___12___, if you really want to give it up,
you can still do it. Doing exercise and getting more
___13___ are important in helping you stop smoking.
Having enough water and fruit helps, too. You should
also say "no" when you are given a cigarette. Remember
to ask your friends not to smoke around ___14___.
And tell yourself ___15___ day that smoking is bad
for your health.

11. (　) ① decide　② forget　③ remember　④ stop
12. (　) ① Besides　② Finally　③ However　④ So
13. (　) ① credit　② money　③ rest　④ trouble
14. (　) ① here　② there　③ themselves　④ you
15. (　) ① a　② every　③ one　④ some

Joe got up and was thirsty. He went to the ___16___ and wanted to make a cold drink for himself. On the shelf there were a lot of bottles. He looked from left to right and found a ___17___. "Lemon Juice !" he saw two ___18___ happily. He put some in the water and drank a whole glass. It ___19___ terrible and he felt sick. "What's wrong ?" asked his brother, Bill. Joe told him about the lemon juice. "Lemon Juice ?" Bill picked up the bottle and laughed loudly, "Can't you ___20___ ?" It says : Detergent with Real Lemon Juice.

16. (　) ① bathroom　② bedroom
　　　　③ kitchen　④ living room
17. (　) ① bottle　② glass　③ shelf　④ wok
18. (　) ① bottles　② glasses　③ lemons　④ words
19. (　) ① looked　② smelled　③ sounded　④ tasted
20. (　) ① listen　② read　③ speak　④ write

Cats and dogs have different ways of showing their feelings. If a dog barks, you know someone is at the door of your ___21___ . But cats never do that. Although both of them wag their tails, it means ___22___ feelings. If a dog wags its tail, you know it's ___23___ . However, when a cat wags its tail, it is angry. They also ___24___ their owners. It is a way dogs show their love for the owner. But not for cats. If cats lick your hand, they just want to eat the salt on the hand. Nothing more. To show they ___25___ you, they may sit on your head.

21. (　　) ① house　　② office　　③ school　　④ store
22. (　　) ① different　② similar　　③ sweet　　④ true
23. (　　) ① angry　　② happy　　③ sad　　④ tired
24. (　　) ① bark　　② bite　　③ eat　　④ lick
25. (　　) ① believe　② hate　　③ know　　④ love

cigarette 香煙	salt 鹽	detergent 清潔劑
tail 尾巴	juice 汁	wag 搖
lemon 檸檬	whole 完整的	

八十二年度台灣省暨高雄市公立高中聯招試題

A 請仔細閱讀下面文章，選出最適當的答案，使句意完整。

Everyone has his own dream. But how to make it ___1___ is not easy. Let's take Peter for example. He wanted to be a boss but he came from a poor (貧窮的) family. So, after he ___2___ junior high school, he didn't go to senior high school. ___3___, he became a factory worker. Although he was a factory worker, he worked hard and used every minute to learn new things. After working hard for fifteen years, he ___4___ became the boss of a factory. It is true that hard work ___5___ success and Peter is a good example.

1. (　) ① to come true ② come true
　　　 ③ coming true ④ came true

2. (　) ① graduated from ② came from
　　　 ③ returned to ④ returned from

3. (　) ① Besides ② Instead ③ Especially ④ Also

4. (　) ① real ② certain ③ finally ④ suddenly

5. (　) ① takes ② grows ③ needs ④ brings

B 請仔細閱讀下面文章，將最適當的一個字填入空格中。

Many people who enjoy watching or reading about sports do not play them. They may not have the ___6___ for them because they are too busy. They may not have the e ___7___ y for them because they are too tired after work. Maybe they played them ten or twenty years ___8___ , but not now. Besides, they may not ___9___ able to play the sports they like. For example, thousands ___10___ girls and women watch baseball games, but there are few woman baseball teams.

6. _____

7. _____

8. _____

9. _____

10. _____

My father loves trees very much. He often says that plants can make our ___11___ fresh and keep the sun away in summer. However, he lives in the city and ___12___ is not much space for him to ___13___ trees. So he ___14___ care of the trees in our neighborhood. I think it is a good idea that we are interested not only in our ___15___ things but also in things shared by everyone.

11. _____

12. _____

13. _____

14. _____

15. _____

八十二年度北區五年制專科學校聯招試題

A 請仔細閱讀下面文章，選出最適當的答案，使句意完整。

Peter : You don't look very good. Did something
  _____1_____ ? Are you all right?

 Bob : No, I'm not. That English test was really
  _____2_____ . I didn't do very well.

Peter : That doesn't _____3_____ me.

 Bob : Why not?

Peter : I usually study some every morning. You always
  do all of _____4_____ studying at the last minute.

 Bob : I know, but I don't like studying English. It
  certainly _____5_____ .

1. (　　) ① wrong　　② happened　　③ happen　　④ special
2. (　　) ① hardly　　② more easier　　③ easily　　④ hard
3. (　　) ① start　　② free　　③ surprise　　④ record
4. (　　) ① his　　② my　　③ her　　④ your
5. (　　) ① cheers me up a lot　　② bores me a lot
  ③ gives me a hand　　④ makes me good

　　Mr. Martin is a writer and _____6_____ a lot of money
by writing stories. He likes _____7_____ stories better than
writing true _____8_____ . He does not have to spend time
finding out _____9_____ , for example, names and dates. Many
people like to buy the stories _____10_____ he makes up.

6. (　　) ① makes　② lends　③ having　④ putting

7. (　　) ① make up　　　② making up
　　　　　③ give up　　　④ giving up

8. (　　) ① one　② ones　③ own　④ owns

9. (　　) ① facts　② exercises　③ neighbors　④ forests

10. (　　) ① where　② who　③ when　④ which

　　　　　__11__ what to buy today is much harder. Some
__12__ are very glad when they have many choices.
__13__ get tired __14__ trying to choose the right
product. There are also buyers who __15__ because
there are too many similar products.

11. (　　) ① Choose　　　② Chose
　　　　　③ Choice　　　④ Choosing

12. (　　) ① shoppers　　② teams
　　　　　③ presents　　④ strangers

13. (　　) ① Other　　　② The other
　　　　　③ Others　　　④ Another

14. (　　) ① out　② of　③ down　④ off

15. (　　) ① got confusing　　② get confused
　　　　　③ seemed confusing　④ seems confused

八十二年度中區五年制專科學校聯招試題

A 請仔細閱讀下面文章，選出最適當的答案，使句意完整。

One day the lion was ___1___ in a net. The little mouse went to help him. He started to bite the net. In a short time the great animal was ___2___.

1. (　) ① complained　　② catched
　　　③ caught　　　　④ counted
2. (　) ① broken　　　　② pronounced
　　　③ troubled　　　④ freed

They are building a new office building across the ___3___, and the workers never stop ___4___! Our little garden is always filled with dust and dirt. When it rains there is ___5___ everywhere.

3. (　) ① country　② story　③ stationery　④ street
4. (　) ① digging　② discovery　③ exciting　④ drinking
5. (　) ① machine　② mud　③ mail　④ match

All students need to have good study habits. If we have ___6___ good habits, we can learn things quickly. Living room is not a good place for us to study in because it is often too noisy. It is better to study in the bedroom ___7___ of the living room. Before we study, be sure to clean our desk and get a good desk light on it. If we have too many things on the desk, we will feel ___8___ and get confused easily. Then we just can not study well.

6. (　　) ① so   　② other   　③ some   　④ much
7. (　　) ① during ② instead ③ then   ④ than
8. (　　) ① tiring ② tire   ③ tires   ④ tired

The man who ___9___ on the second floor is neither young nor healthy. He has trouble ___10___ , so you have to throw his newspaper up to his apartment.

9. (　　) ① lives 　② live   　③ lived   ④ living
10. (　　) ① walk 　② walking ③ to walk ④ walked

Mr. Lin likes making up stories. Many people like to buy the stories which he makes up. His stories are very ___11___ and people always enjoy ___12___ them.

11. (　　) ① interesting   　② interest
　　　　 ③ interested   　④ interests
12. (　　) ① to read ② read   ③ reads ④ reading

Alice works in an office. She uses a typewriter. She is a secretary. She never works ___13___ night, nor does she ever work ___14___ Sunday. ___15___, she is never late for work. She is really a good worker.

13. (　　) ① in　　② on　　③ at　　④ for
14. (　　) ① in　　② on　　③ at　　④ for
15. (　　) ① Just now　　② Right here
　　　　　③ Neither　　　④ However

八十二年度南區五年制專科學校聯招試題

A 請仔細閱讀下面文章，選出最適當的答案，使句意完整。

Life was ___1___ harder than it is today. Modern living is more comfortable, but it ___2___ pollution problems. Air pollution, for example, is ___3___ the biggest and the worst kind of pollution. Many countries are trying hard. However, still a lot of things need ___4___ to save our world. Everyone must help. For example, if fewer people drive cars, there will be ___5___ pollution and better traffic.

1. (　　) ① more ② much
   　　　 ③ much more ④ very

2. (　　) ① bringing ② has bring
   　　　 ③ has brought ④ is brought

3. (　　) ① becoming ② became
   　　　 ③ become ④ to becoming

4. (　　) ① to do ② be done
   　　　 ③ to have done ④ to be done

5. (　　) ① fewer ② more ③ less ④ much

八十二年度台北市公立高職聯招試題

A 請仔細閱讀下面文章，選出最適當的答案，使句意完整。

A year has four ____1____ . They are spring, summer, fall, and winter. Spring is ____2____ season of the year. Summer is very ____3____ . It comes ____4____ spring. Fall comes before winter. It is ____5____ in winter.

1. (　　) ① days　② weeks　③ months　④ seasons
2. (　　) ① the last　　　② the third
　　　　③ the second　　④ the first
3. (　　) ① warm　② hot　③ cool　④ cold
4. (　　) ① after　② with　③ into　④ before
5. (　　) ① warm　② hot　③ cool　④ cold

There are several ____6____ in a year, but I like ____7____ most. During that time, sons and ____8____ always go home and are together with ____9____ parents. People visit friends, usually bringing red envelopes（紅包） ____10____ money in them for the children.

6. (　　) ① weeks　② holidays　③ seasons　④ months
7. (　　) ① Teacher's Day　　② Youth Day
　　　　③ Christmas Day　　④ the Chinese New Year
8. (　　) ① teachers　② daughters　③ doctors　④ nurses
9. (　　) ① his　② her　③ their　④ your
10. (　　) ① in　② on　③ have　④ with

Joe has a very good friend, Ken, _____11_____ can speak several languages. Ken's _____12_____ is very good. _____13_____ their last vacation, they traveled around America together. Joe could _____14_____ talk with Americans nor make himself understood. After they came back, Joe studied English hard. Now he can speak it _____15_____ and even sing some English songs.

11. (　　) ① which ② that ③ whom ④ who
12. (　　) ① pronunciation ② bridge
　　　　　③ school ④ tool
13. (　　) ① At ② On ③ With ④ From
14. (　　) ① either ② neither ③ both ④ but
15. (　　) ① lazily ② noisily ③ well ④ sadly

八十二年度台灣省暨高雄市公立高職聯招試題

A 請仔細閱讀下面文章，選出最適當的答案，使句意完整。

Betty : Mary, would you like to help me pack?

Mary : Yes, I'd be ____1____ to.

Betty : Would you ____2____ me your backpack?

Mary : Of course. And you should ____3____ your sweater.

Betty : I would.

Mary : Did you forget ____4____ your swimsuit?

Betty : No, I didn't. But mine is ____5____ small now.

Mary : Would you like to borrow mine?

Betty : Thank you very much.

1. ( ) ① sorry ② bored ③ tired ④ happy
2. ( ) ① lend ② have ③ catch ④ borrow
3. ( ) ① hold ② take ③ make ④ lose
4. ( ) ① pack ② packs ③ packed ④ to pack
5. ( ) ① how ② much ③ too ④ more

Peter Wang, Bill Lin and Steve Huang are all farmers. Peter ____6____ tangerines, Bill grows ____7____, and Steve grows vegetables. Peter, Bill and Steve ____8____ what they grow. Peter sells tangerines ____9____ winter, Bill sells oranges in fall, ____10____ Steve sells vegetables in summer. They all work especially hard in the growing season.

6. (　　) ① makes　　② picks　　③ grows　　④ catches
7. (　　) ① vegetables　② plants　③ flowers　④ oranges
8. (　　) ① sell　　② sells　　③ sold　　④ selling
9. (　　) ① on　　② at　　③ in　　④ of
10. (　　) ① so　　② and　　③ or　　④ when

八十一年度台北市公立高中聯招試題

A 請仔細閱讀下面文章，選出最適當的答案，使句意完整。

I often dream about living in Disney's dream city. There, a computer controls everything in the ____1____. You don't need a ____2____ to open the door. When you put a special card in a hole next to it, it opens by ____3____. If you tell the computer the time for your breakfast, your food will be ____4____ after you get up. It is easy for everyone to breathe because there is no ____5____ pollution. It'll be really nice to live in such a city.

1. (   ) ① cap   ② house   ③ office   ④ school
2. (   ) ① book   ② box   ③ key   ④ plug
3. (   ) ① itself   ② myself   ③ ourselves   ④ yourself
4. (   ) ① delicious   ② finished
         ③ ready   ④ satisfying
5. (   ) ① air   ② noise   ③ trash   ④ water

Mrs. Wang took her son, Paul, to a doctor. She was worried about him because he was ____6____ than other boys. The doctor ____7____ him carefully and gave him some medicine.

"The medicine will make Paul feel ____8____ ," the doctor said, "but he will become taller and stronger."

After Paul took the medicine, he really started to ____9____ a lot when he had free time. His mother was ____10____ again. Should Paul keep taking the medicine?

6. (　) ① heavier　② lazier　③ quieter　④ smaller

7. (　) ① looked at　　　　② looked for
　　　　③ looked like　　　④ thought about

8. (　) ① angry　② hungry　③ sad　④ thirsty

9. (　) ① eat　② play　③ rest　④ study

10. (　) ① deceit　② happy　③ sick　④ troubled

Many people now think that teachers give students too many tests in class and too much ____11____ after school. So children do not have any ____12____ for other activities. ____13____ teachers and parents talk to each other about the problem they could work on it together. Teachers should try to make the tests easier and ____14____ the homework better. ____15____ , parents should help their children develop good study habits. Then, the students will become happier and healthier.

11. (　　) ① convenience　　② exercise
　　　　　 ③ homework　　　 ④ noise

12. (　　) ① money　② space　③ time　④ trouble

13. (　　) ① Although　② Because　③ If　④ Only

14. (　　) ① create　② finish　③ plan　④ write

15. (　　) ① Besides　② Finally　③ However　④ Instead

People often complain about buses in Taipei. The ___16___ from the buses pollutes our city. Buses are usually full of people and it's hard to get a ___17___. Sometimes people have to wait for a long time but the bus doesn't come. And, some bus drivers stop the bus ___18___, so, if people on the bus are not careful, they may fall down and get hurt. It is ___19___ that not so many people like to go to places by bus.

If the bus service (服務) can be made better, there will be ___20___ traffic problems. Then people will feel it convenient to go anywhere in the city.

16. (　　) ① mud　② smoke　③ trash　④ water

17. (　　) ① chair　② seat　③ ticket　④ truck

18. (　　) ① carefully　② noisily　③ slowly　④ suddenly

19. (　　) ① easy　② hard　③ natural　④ surprising

20. (　　) ① a few　② fewer　③ more　④ many

八十一年度台灣省暨高雄市公立高中聯招試題

A 請仔細閱讀下面文章，選出最適當的答案，使句意完整。

Our country has made laws against copying others' ideas. Good ideas ____1____ a lot of time and energy to develop, but they could be copied easily. ____2____, we often don't know that we are breaking the laws. We may copy others' books without asking them first. We may not use the ____3____ computer products. And even when we buy tapes and records, we may be ____4____ the laws because some of them may be copies. Knowing this, we should be very careful when we buy things. Everyone should help to fight copying others' ideas because ____5____ are not enough.

1. (　　) ① take　　② use　　③ spend　　④ waste
2. (　　) ① Carefully　② However　③ Similar　④ Together
3. (　　) ① fresh　　② simple　　③ original　　④ correct
4. (　　) ① ready to　② at　　③ out of　　④ against
5. (　　) ① copies　　② products　　③ laws　　④ ideas

B 請仔細閱讀下面文章，將最適當的一個字填入空格中。

　　(1) watch　　(2) while　　(3) boring　　(4) spend
　　(5) forget　　(6) fun　　(7) in front of　　(8) turn on

Young boys and girls love to watch television. Some children ___6___ about eight hours a day in school and about six hours a day ___7___ the television. Some watch TV ___8___ they are doing their homework. Some even watch TV all the evening and ___9___ to eat dinner. These are all bad habits. It is ___10___ to watch television, but to read a book or to visit friends is fun, too. Young children should not watch too much television.

C 讀完整篇後，請填入適當的字。

Although I often get excited when I have a lot of choices, I find it is not easy to make the best decision. It is much harder to decide what ___11___ do in the future. I hope to be a secretary, but I neither have any idea about the computer nor knew how to use a typewriter. I hope to be a ___12___, but I have trouble speaking before students. I hope to be a writer, but I am not able to ___13___ up stories. Whether I should be a doctor ___14___ not is another problem to me. When I think about this, ___15___ almost go crazy.

11. _____

12. _____

13. _____

14. _____

15. _____

After learning English for several years, many students still can't use it well. Some students can read and write quite well, but they can't ___16___ English, especially to people from other countries. I think this is ___17___ they do not have enough practice. To speak English well, they should often ___18___ to the English programs on the radio and watch good English programs on TV. They should try to practice English ___19___ their English teachers and classmates on their ___20___ . If they do so, they will become more interested in English, and they can learn it better.

16. _____

17. _____

18. _____

19. _____

20. _____

八十一年度北區五年制專科學校聯招試題

A 請仔細閱讀下面文章，選出最適當的答案，使句意完整。

_____1_____ they were leaving the park, they heard a dog barking _____2_____ . Then they saw a man _____3_____ a bicycle very fast. _____4_____ old dog was barking at the man _____5_____ the bicycle.

1. (　　) ① That　　② Which　　③ Where　　④ As
2. (　　) ① noisy　　② quite　　③ noisily　　④ noise
3. (　　) ① riding　　② rode　　③ ridden　　④ rides
4. (　　) ① Those　　② A　　③ These　　④ An
5. (　　) ① into　　② for　　③ on　　④ in

People enjoyed _____6_____ in those days. They did not hurry _____7_____ store to store, but slowly decided to buy what they wanted. Customers and clerks were not only very friendly, but they never got _____8_____ with each other. Many clerks even knew the names of their customers. If they had new products, clerks would show _____9_____ to their customers. _____10_____ what to buy was not hard.

6. (　　) ① shop　　② to shop　　③ shopping　　④ shoping

7. (　　) ① between　② to　　　　③ in　　　　　④ from

8. (　　) ① angry　　② anger　　　③ angrily　　④ angryly

9. (　　) ① it　　　　② they　　　　③ him　　　　④ them

10. (　　) ① Choosing　　　　　② Choose
　　　　　③ Chosen　　　　　　④ Choice

八十一年度中區五年制專科學校聯招試題

A 請仔細閱讀下面文章，選出最適當的答案，使句意完整。

Many people stopped to look at the beautiful flowers. Everyone ____1____ about the trash, but no one picked any of it up. It's not hard to put trash in a trash can. Why are people so ____2____ ?

1. (　) ① throw　② complained　③ cleaned　④ worry
2. (　) ① lake　② thirsty　③ happily　④ lazy

Mr. Chen owned a small fruit ____3____ in the country. He liked nature, and he liked natural things. He used no ____4____ on his fruit and grew it ____5____ .

3. (　) ① cake　② farm　③ juice　④ vegetable
4. (　) ① chemicals　② oranges　③ smoking　④ parking
5. (　) ① sweet　② jelly　③ fresh　④ naturally

Using your free time well is important. Doing healthy activities when you have free time ____6____ more important. Everyone needs activities which ____7____ develop a strong mind and a healthy body.

6. (　) ① are　　　② the　　　③ is　　　④ much
7. (　) ① help　　② helps　　③ helping　④ helped

　　A　language　___8___　is　called　a　dead　language.
Whether　a　language　___9___　anymore　is　not　important.
If　no　one　___10___　it,　however,　a　language　can　not　live
and　grow.

8. (　) ① no use　　　　　② people not use
　　　　③ people use　　　④ people do not use

9. (　) ① is writing　　　② writes
　　　　③ is written　　　④ written

10. (　) ① speaks　　② tells　　③ talks　　④ says

　　When　we　study　correctly　and　get　knowledge　on　our
own,　we　enjoy　___11___　.　We　also　learn　more　and
understand　___12___　.

11. (　) ① learn　　　　　② learning
　　　　③ to learn　　　④ to be learning

12. (　) ① too well　　　② very good
　　　　③ better　　　　④ much best

Betty took Kevin's flashlight without asking first, and then she lost it. She hoped that she wouldn't tell him the truth, and asked Mary ____13____ . "If I were you," said Mary, "I ____14____ tell a lie; I am sure you won't get into trouble, but you ____15____ if you lie."

13. (   ) ① what she should do   ② what should she do
         ③ how she should do   ④ how should she do

14. (   ) ① won't   ② wouldn't   ③ didn't   ④ don't

15. (   ) ① are   ② would   ③ were   ④ will

八十一年度南區五年制專科學校聯招試題

A 請仔細閱讀下面文章，選出最適當的答案，使句意完整。

It was Sunday yesterday. ＿＿1＿＿ all got up early in the morning. At six, Mrs. Wang was busy ＿＿2＿＿ breakfast for her family, and Jean, her daughter, washed the rice and vegetables. After breakfast, Mr. and Mrs. Wang went to visit their friends. Then Jean ＿＿3＿＿ listening to the radio and washing her skirts. After that, she ＿＿4＿＿ her skirts; ＿＿5＿＿ , she burned them. Finally, she studied English until her parents came back.

1. (　　) ① Wangs   ② The Wangs
       ③ The Wang   ④ Wang

2. (　　) ① cooking ② to cook   ③ cook   ④ cooked

3. (　　) ① liked   ② remembered ③ started ④ forgot

4. (　　) ① made   ② ironed   ③ did   ④ worked

5. (　　) ① though   ② that   ③ when   ④ however

Many students will have a lot of free time during summer vacation. They are very excited about ＿＿6＿＿ coming because they can do many activities which are ＿＿7＿＿ to them during summer vacation. Tom and Kevin ＿＿8＿＿ plans for their summer vacation. Tom will go camping with his family, and Kevin will have a lot of fun _____9_____ his English with his American pen pal.

All students can have a happy summer like Tom and Kevin if they use their time well and make their plans _____10_____ .

6. (　　) ① its　　　② their　　　③ whose　　　④ his

7. (　　) ① interested　　　② confused
　　　③ interesting　　　④ confusing

8. (　　) ① had already made　　　② make already
　　　③ have already made　　　④ has already made

9. (　　) ① to practice　　　② practicing
　　　③ practiced　　　④ practice

10. (　　) ① quick　② quickly　③ careful　④ carefully

八十一年度台北區公立高職聯招試題

A 請仔細閱讀下面文章，選出最適當的答案，使句意完整。

The Huangs live in an apartment which has only two bedrooms. Because they have another ____1____ now, they need a ____2____ apartment with ____3____ bedrooms. They are going to ____4____ the old apartment and ____5____ to a new one.

1. (　　) ① dog 　　② child 　　③ car 　　④ good friend
2. (　　) ① beautiful ② small 　　③ modern ④ big
3. (　　) ① many 　　② few 　　③ three 　　④ some
4. (　　) ① sold 　　② sell 　　③ buy 　　④ bought
5. (　　) ① move 　　② buy 　　③ go 　　④ moved

There are five people in the Wang family, ____6____ like going camping on holidays. ____7____ their last vacation, they camped at the beach and ____8____ a good time there. They took many pictures. In one picture, they are catching fish. And in all ____9____ pictures, they are playing ____10____ happily.

6. (　　) ① which 　② that 　　③ whom 　　④ who
7. (　　) ① During ② At 　　③ Before 　④ Near
8. (　　) ① have 　② had 　　③ are 　　④ were

9. (　　) ① some　② other　③ another　④ the other
10. (　　) ① a volleyball　　② volleyballs
　　　　　③ volleyball　　　④ with volleyball

Every year many groups hold ___11___ activities for young people. These activities are usually quite ___12___. Some of the best activities are ___13___ by the China Youth Corps. When young people ___14___ the CYC's programs, they are ___15___.

11. (　　) ① delicious　　② special
　　　　　③ comfortable　④ instant
12. (　　) ① interest　　② interests
　　　　　③ interested　④ interesting
13. (　　) ① held　② hold　③ holding　④ to hold
14. (　　) ① run　② take　③ join　④ have
15. (　　) ① excite　② excites　③ excited　④ exciting

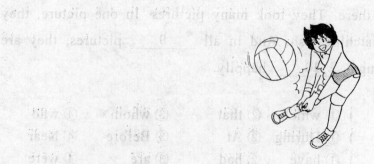

八十一年度台灣省暨高雄市公立高職聯招試題

A 請仔細閱讀下面文章，選出最適當的答案，使句意完整。

Tom is a high school student. He likes to play the guitar. He has an old guitar, but he wants to have ___1___ .

Last Monday was a fine day. Tom got up ___2___ he usually did. After breakfast, he ___3___ and walked to school. On his way to school, he found a bag ___4___ and ___5___ . There was a lot of money inside it. He thought, "Nobody saw me. If I had the money, my dream would ___6___ , and I can have a new guitar."

After school, Tom hurried home. He wasn't happy. His mother told him to ___7___ his shoes and jacket and take a bath. She saw the bag and the money. His mother knew that he might ___8___ . She said, "Tom, as long as you ___9___ , you will be a good boy." They took the money to the police station. A police officer said to Tom, "You are a very ___10___ boy."

1. (　　) ① a new tool　　② a new one
　　　　 ③ some help　　④ some new ideas

2. (　　) ① as early as　　　② as well as
　　　　　③ late　　　　　　④ faster

3. (　　) ① got dressed　　　② sat down
　　　　　③ came in　　　　　④ went to bed

4. (　　) ① on the bus　　　　② on the train
　　　　　③ on the ground　　④ at home

5. (　　) ① put it down　　　② picked it up
　　　　　③ took it away　　　④ made it up

6. (　　) ① look up　　　　　② run away
　　　　　③ find out　　　　　④ come true

7. (　　) ① take off　　　　　② put on
　　　　　③ turn on　　　　　④ go away

8. (　　) ① run out of gas　　② give up plans
　　　　　③ get hurt　　　　　④ get into trouble

9. (　　) ① tell a lie　　　　 ② make mistakes
　　　　　③ tell the truth　　④ try again

10. (　　) ① lazy　　② noise　　③ honest　　④ cold

八十年度台北市公立高中聯招試題

A 請仔細閱讀下面文章，選出最適當的答案，使句意完整。

The weather in Taipei often changes fast. It changes so fast every ___1___ that many people catch a cold ___2___ in hot summer. Some people leave their houses in the morning ___3___ enough clothes. When they come home in the evening, they don't feel good.

Sue caught a cold yesterday. She was too ___4___ to go to school. Her mother took her to a ___5___. He wanted her to take some medicine and drink a lot of water.

1. (　　) ① day　　② week　　③ month　　④ year
2. (　　) ① while　　② even　　③ again　　④ only
3. (　　) ① in　　② not　　③ with　　④ without
4. (　　) ① poor　　② cold　　③ lazy　　④ weak
5. (　　) ① hospital　② teacher　③ doctor　④ visitor

Some people do not use their time well. Sometimes they are very lazy. They are not ___6___ workers and often make many mistakes. They often do their work and ___7___ other things at the same time.

Mr. Lin is this kind of person. All week his family talked about going to the country ___8___. But on Saturday, he went to work in the morning. He made several big mistakes and did his work three ___9___. When he went home very late, his wife and children were very angry ___10___ did not talk to him.

6. (　　) ① slow and stupid 　② brave and smart
　　　　 ③ proud and popular ④ quick and careful
7. (　　) ① fill up 　　　　　② think about
　　　　 ③ find out 　　　　　④ put on
8. (　　) ① during the week 　② during the summer
　　　　 ③ on the weekend 　 ④ before the New Year
9. (　　) ① times 　② hours 　③ months 　④ holidays
10. (　　) ① so 　　② who 　　③ and 　　　④ but

　　A little girl and her mother were walking in the country when it suddenly began to rain. They didn't have their umbrellas with them so they were soon _____11_____, and the little girl didn't feel very happy.

　　While they were walking home through the rain, the girl was thinking. _____12_____ she turned to her mother and said to her, "Why does it rain, Mother? It's not good."

　　"No, it isn't very good, but it _____13_____ a lot," answered her mother. "It rains to make rice and vegetables _____14_____ for us and if it doesn't rain for a long time, trees will _____15_____."

　　The girl thought about this for a few seconds and then she asked, "Why does it rain on the road too, Mother?"

11. (　　) ① tired 　　② sad 　　　③ wet 　　④ sick
12. (　　) ① Naturally ② Easily 　③ Finally 　④ Happily
13. (　　) ① costs 　　② helps 　　③ washes 　④ rains
14. (　　) ① grow 　　② develop 　③ hold 　　④ go
15. (　　) ① cry 　　　② die 　　　③ break 　　④ move

Linda is a woman with a kind heart. She always spends part of her free time ___16___ something she thinks good. Now since her children have grown up, she has ___17___ free time to do what she wants to. She knows that some people may need help ___18___ they get out of the hospital. She finds their names and ___19___ with them when they are ready to go home.

After they get home, she buys food, cooks it, and talks with them as they ___20___. She does other things for them, too. Linda has helped many people this way. It's a good job for her.

16. (　) ① buying　② cooking　③ making　④ doing
17. (　) ① little　② less　③ some　④ more
18. (　) ① before　② since　③ after　④ until
19. (　) ① sits　② talks　③ goes　④ plays
20. (　) ① eat　② read　③ study　④ sleep

八十年度台灣省暨高雄市公立高中聯招試題

A 請仔細閱讀下面文章，選出最適當的答案，使句意完整。

Usually typhoons hit Taiwan between June and ___1___ , the eighth month of the year. When a typhoon comes, it brings both strong winds and heavy rain. It is bad for farm ___2___ . So people have to pay more money for vegetables. It is dangerous to go out on a typhoon day. We might be hit by a falling tree. ___3___ like mountain climbing or swimming at the ___4___ may not be held. Sometimes we may have no light in the night because there may be no ___5___ .

1. (　　) ① August　　　　　② September
　　　　　③ October　　　　　④ February
2. (　　) ① animals　② package　③ pork　④ products
3. (　　) ① Activities ② Picnics　③ Subjects　④ Things
4. (　　) ① ground　② balcony　③ beach　④ forest
5. (　　) ① water　　　　　　② electricity
　　　　　③ earthquake　　　④ thundershower

If you want to learn English well, you must ___6___ a good dictionary. It is an important tool. When you find a new word in a lesson, be sure to ___7___ in the dictionary. Don't be afraid of the troubles. A dictionary will ___8___ what the word means but also how it is used. Of course, it will show you how to pronounce words ___9___ you can read them loudly. Most important, you have to read the sentences which ___10___ in the dictionary.

6. (　　) ① have　　② had　　③ to have　　④ having

7. (　　) ① pick it up　　② give it up
　　　　③ make it up　　④ look it up

8. (　　) ① only not tell you　　② tell you not only
　　　　③ tell not only you　　④ not tell only you

9. (　　) ① as long as　　② no matter when
　　　　③ so that　　④ since

10. (　　) ① to list　　② are listed
　　　　③ are listing　　④ have listed

B 請仔細閱讀下面文章，將最適當的一個字填入空格中。

　　(1) less and less　　(2) come true　　(3) breathe
　　(4) more and more　　(5) turn off　　(6) give up
　　(7) many cars　　(8) much traffic

Air pollution is the most serious kind of pollution. There is too ___11___ on the streets and there are too many factories near the city. Besides, many people smoke. All these make air pollution ___12___ serious. If we don't do anything to fight it, we will have no fresh air to ___13___ . Many trees will die and many people will get sick. We hope that more people ___14___ smoking and fewer people drive. Then our dream of having a cleaner place will ___15___ .

(1) confused   (2) satisfied   (3) seem to
(4) cannot   (5) when   (6) until
(7) a day   (8) some day

Today people spend much more money on food than before. In the past, people would feel _____16_____ if they had enough to eat. Today in the supermarkets people have all kinds of food to choose. There may be a convenience store near your home. It is open twenty-four hours _____17_____ . You can buy a sandwich or a hamburger there _____18_____ you feel hungry. In the cities there are lots of nice restaurants which are crowded with people. They _____19_____ care nothing about spending so much money in eating. Eating is important, but we should not forget that our minds also need a kind of food. That is knowledge. We _____20_____ get knowledge without reading books. So why don't we go into a bookstore after we get out of a restaurant?

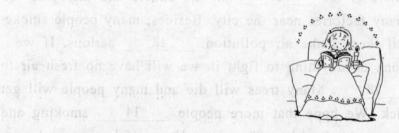

八十年度北區五年制專科學校聯招試題

A 請仔細閱讀下面文章，選出最適當的答案，使句意完整。

If you want to be ＿＿＿1＿＿＿, you must take ＿＿＿2＿＿＿ every day. Running and swimming are good ＿＿＿3＿＿＿ to build a strong body. Besides, if you want to develop your mind, you must read. In the library, there are lots of different kinds of ＿＿＿4＿＿＿ which you can read in it. Also, you can borrow books which ＿＿＿5＿＿＿ you.

1. (　　) ① sick 　　② magic 　　③ healthy 　　④ weak
2. (　　) ① battle 　　② exercise 　　③ game 　　④ wheel
3. (　　) ① activities ② exams 　　③ products 　④ umbrella
4. (　　) ① trains 　　　　　　② elephants
　　　　③ calendars 　　　　④ magazines
5. (　　) ① interest 　② change 　③ speak 　　④ dig

Last Monday, Tom got a headache. Then he decided ＿＿＿6＿＿＿ his doctor and have a checkup. After he walked into the hospital, a nurse asked him to write his name and things about him on a piece of paper. He did it as ＿＿＿7＿＿＿ as he could. While he was waiting for his doctor, he complained ＿＿＿8＿＿＿ his headache. The nurse cheered him ＿＿＿9＿＿＿ and ＿＿＿10＿＿＿ him not to worry about it.

6. (　) ① see ② seeing ③ seen ④ to see
7. (　) ① long ② late ③ fast ④ proud
8. (　) ① to ② about ③ in ④ for
9. (　) ① down ② on ③ for ④ up
10. (　) ① telling ② told ③ to tell ④ had told

Each one ___11___ his own study habit. ___12___ is very hard to change his habit. Joe is a student who usually studies in the library. ___13___ the library is open, Joe spends most of his time there on the weekend. Frank, Joe's friend, is a worker who likes to study after work, especially before ___14___ to bed. He thinks it is quiet during the night. Besides, he always has a problem of finding a parking space around the library, so that is ___15___ Frank likes to study at home.

11. (　) ① have ② is ③ are ④ has
12. (　) ① There ② That ③ This ④ It
13. (　) ① No matter how ② As long as
　　　　 ③ So ④ Before
14. (　) ① going ② to go ③ went ④ go
15. (　) ① what ② where ③ why ④ how

八十年度中區五年制專科學校聯招試題

A 請仔細閱讀下面文章，選出最適當的答案，使句意完整。

There are not any ____1____ subjects; there are only ____2____ people. When people ask questions and try to learn about a subject on their own, they will become more ____3____ in it.

1. (　　) ① boring or interested　　② boring or interesting
　　　　 ③ bored or interesting　　④ bored or interested

2. (　　) ① boring or interested　　② boring or interesting
　　　　 ③ bored or interesting　　④ bored or interested

3. (　　) ① interest　　　　　　　② interesting
　　　　 ③ interested　　　　　　④ interests

In the ____4____ , or in a smaller city, there are not so many large stores or shops. There are also ____5____ supermarkets.

4. (　　) ① nation　　② world　　③ mountain　　④ country
5. (　　) ① few　　　② a few　　③ many　　　④ much

Many people enjoy ____6____ when they have free time. They like going to the library. There they can read books or magazines ____7____ interest them.

6. (　) ① read　② to read　③ reading　④ reads
7. (　) ① what　② which　③ who　④ whom

Food ＿＿＿8＿＿＿ is more convenient today. If people do not have time to make lunch, they ＿＿＿9＿＿＿ a sandwich ＿＿＿10＿＿＿ a convenience store.

8. (　) ① shop　② shops　③ shopped　④ shopping
9. (　) ① could buy　　② could have bought
　　　　③ can buy　　　④ can have bought
10. (　) ① at　② for　③ to　④ with

八十年度南區五年制專科學校聯招試題

A 請仔細閱讀下面文章，選出最適當的答案，使句意完整。

Today many people enjoy city life. Life in a big city is always more ___1___ and convenient. People can not only go to those important games played by their ___2___ teams, but also visit the ___3___ very often. However, city life has also brought new problems. We all know that pollution is one of the ___4___ of modern city life. People seldom ___5___ fresh air in big cities. So, living in a big city has its good and bad sides.

1. (　　) ① clean ② easy
　　　 ③ quiet ④ comfortable
2. (　　) ① latest ② favorite
　　　 ③ dangerous ④ instant
3. (　　) ① museums ② music
　　　 ③ nature ④ bathrooms
4. (　　) ① grounds ② hearts ③ programs ④ products
5. (　　) ① affect ② practice ③ breathe ④ breath

Jimmy owned a fruit farm in the country. Every morning he drove his car ___6___ fruit to the market in town. Chemicals ___7___ on Jimmy's fruit. It was

_____8_____ any other fruit in the market, _____9_____ not many people cared about this. Because the fruit was a little expensive, most people didn't want to buy it. Jimmy was making less and less money, and he got confused. However, Jimmy was an honest man, and money wasn't everything to him. _____10_____ how much he lost, he would not use chemicals on his fruit.

6. (　　) ① fill up with   ② full of
         ③ in back of   ④ proud of

7. (　　) ① never be used   ② never used
         ③ have never used   ④ were never used

8. (　　) ① very healthy than   ② much healthy than
         ③ healthier than   ④ more healthier than

9. (　　) ① but   ② so   ③ if   ④ or

10. (　　) ① No more   ② No matter
         ③ No sooner   ④ No longer

You Can
CALL Me

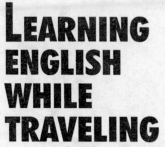

|||||||||||||||||||| ● 學習出版公司門市部 ● ||||||||||||||||||||

台北地區：台北市許昌街 10 號 2 樓 TEL：(02)3314060．3319209
台中地區：台中市綠川東街 32 號 8 樓 23 室
　　　　　TEL：(04)2232838

|||||||||||||||||||||||||||||||||||||||||||||||||||||||||||

國中英語 100 分克漏字測驗

編　　著/王榮一
發　行　所/學習出版有限公司　　　　　☎(02) 7045525
郵 撥 帳 號/0512727-2 學習出版社帳戶
登　記　證/局版台業 2179 號
印　刷　所/裕強彩色印刷有限公司
台 北 門 市/台北市許昌街 10 號 2F　　☎(02) 3314060．3319209
台 中 門 市/台中市綠川東街 32 號 8F 23 室　☎(04) 2232838
台灣總經銷/學英文化事業公司　　　　☎(02) 2187307
美國總經銷/Evergreen Book Store　　☎(818) 2813622

售價：新台幣一百五十元正

1997 年 2 月 1 日二版一刷

ISBN 957-519-108-0